Mathematics for Every Student

A series edited by Carol E. Malloy

Mathematics for Every Student

Responding to Diversity, Grades 6–8

Volume Editor

Mark W. Ellis
California State University, Fullerton
Fullerton, California

Series Editor

Carol E. Malloy
University of North Carolina at Chapel Hill
Chapel Hill, North Carolina

NATIONAL COUNCIL OF
TEACHERS OF MATHEMATICS

Library of Congress Cataloging-in-Publication Data

Mathematics for every student. Responding to diversity, grades 6–8 / volume editor, Mark W. Ellis.
p. cm. — (Mathematics for every student series)
ISBN 978-0-87353-612-7
1. Mathematics—Study and teaching (Middle school)—United States. 2. Multicultural education—United States. 3. Educational equalization—United States. I. Ellis, Mark W. (Mark William), 1969– II. National Council of Teachers of Mathematics. III. Title: Responding to diversity, grades 6–8.
QA13.M3545 2008
510.71'273—dc22

2008032086

The National Council of Teachers of Mathematics is a public voice of mathematics education, providing vision, leadership, and professional development to support teachers in ensuring equitable mathematics learning of the highest quality for all students.

Printed in the United States of America

Contents

Contents—*Continued*

Preface

The National Council of Teachers of Mathematics (NCTM) has demonstrated its dedication to equity in the mathematics education of *every student* through its publications, through regional and annual meeting programs, and through professional development programs. In clarification of what is meant by every student, in 1990 the NCTM Board of Directors endorsed the following statement, which set the mathematical education of every child as the goal for mathematics teaching at all levels.

> As a professional organization and as individuals within that organization, the Board of Directors sees the comprehensive mathematics education of every child as its most compelling goal.
>
> By "every child" we mean specifically—
>
> - students who have been denied access in any way to educational opportunities as well as those who have not;
> - students who are African American, Hispanic, American Indian, and other minorities as well as those who are considered to be a part of the majority;
> - students who are female as well as those who are male; and
> - students who have not been successful in school and in mathematics as well as those who have been successful.
>
> It is essential that schools and communities accept the goal of mathematical education for every child. However, this does not mean that every child will have the same interests or capabilities in mathematics. It does mean that we will have to examine our fundamental expectations about what children can learn and can do and that we will have to strive to create learning environments in which raised expectations for children can be met. (NCTM 1991, p. 4)

Through the Equity Principle in *Principles and Standards for School Mathematics* (2000), NCTM built on the challenging goal of the "every child" statement above and extended its vision of equity by stating, "Excellence in mathematics education requires equity—high expectations and strong support for all students" (p. 12). Specifically, the principle states that equity requires high expectations and worthwhile opportunities for all, requires accommodating differences to help everyone learn mathematics, and requires resources and support for all classrooms and all students (pp. 12–14). Guided by the Equity Principle and the charge of the NCTM Educational Materials Committee, the editors of this three-book series are pleased to feature instructional practices of teachers from diverse classrooms that embody this principle and the every-child statement.

The editors would like to thank the authors, who were willing to share their experiences and successful strategies for teaching all students in diverse classrooms; the numerous reviewers for their contributions; and the NCTM Publications Department for their support, patience, and encouragement from our initial meeting through the publication phases of this project. I personally want to thank the volume editors, who worked tirelessly during the development of this series. It was a pleasure and an intellectual inspiration to work with them. They were my friends, critics, and colleagues.

—*Carol E. Malloy*
Series Editor

REFERENCES

National Council of Teachers of Mathematics (NCTM). *Professional Standards for Teaching Mathematics*. Reston, Va.: NCTM, 1991.

———. *Principles and Standards for School Mathematics*. Reston, Va.: NCTM, 2000.

Introduction

We are teachers, teachers of mathematics. Every year we are excited to meet the new students who are placed in our classrooms to learn about mathematics. On the first day of school as we look around the room at their faces, we know that every student has the ability to learn mathematics. At the same time, students look to our faces for guidance through the mathematics content and to their mathematical understanding. Students' confidence in our skills is both our inspiration and our challenge, especially because we know, as Bobbie Poole stated in *I Am a Teacher* (Marquis and Sachs 1990, p. 20),

> Every kid is different. What's exciting is to try to meet the needs of those individual kids. It is never boring. It is different from minute to minute, and there is no formula that works for everyone.

Knowing that no one strategy will work for all students, teachers have the responsibility to determine strategies, both affective and cognitive, that together support all students as they learn mathematics. Affective behaviors—which include students' beliefs about mathematics and self, teachers' beliefs, students' emotions, and students' attitudes—play a prominent role in achievement (McLeod 1991). In the vignette that follows, I describe a situation that I experienced with a student, Alfred, who because of lack of confidence in his academic skills was a behavioral challenge in my mathematics class.

Teachers have the responsibility to determine strategies, both affective and cognitive, that together support all students as they learn mathematics.

Building Confidence through Caring

In my sixth year of teaching, my husband and I moved to a city where he was hired as a central office school administrator. During my interview for a teaching position in the district, the personnel officer encouraged me to take a position at Jefferson High School. She called Jefferson High an inner-city high school whose quality was decreasing. I decided to take that position. When I entered school the first day that students attended, I was nervous. I am always nervous on the first day, but this situation was different. In some ways I was a little scared because in my limited experience as a teacher, I had never taught in a school labeled "inner city." As a result of my preconceived notions of inner-city schools, I had visions of disruptive, unruly, and unmotivated students in the halls and in my classes.

The students I greeted at the door of my classroom were not disruptive or unruly. They were polite, very well dressed, and enthusiastic, and they seemed to be excited to be in my mathematics classes. I learned quickly that this school and its students were similar to the schools where I had previously taught—a normal school with a diverse student population. I was comfortable. But in every perfect situation, an enigma can arise. My enigma the first few days of school was Alfred[1]. He was a rather large

1. This is a pseudonym.

It became apparent that Alfred was testing me and my ability to both control the class and teach algebra.

tenth-grade boy who was enrolled in Algebra Concepts 2—the second year of a two-year course in algebra 1. In the first few days of class, it became apparent that Alfred was testing me and my ability to both control the class and teach algebra. Even though Alfred did not always have his homework ready for class, he did not refuse to do his work. His ability and motivation to complete class work were not the problem; it was his behavior. He was disruptive, sarcastic, and in some situations demeaning to other students. Considering this conduct, I was not sure of a strategy to use to diffuse his need to challenge both the other students and me and to help him become serious about learning algebra.

After thinking for several days, I decided that I would demonstrate through my behavior that Alfred was special to me. I decided to say something special to him every day as he entered the room. Because this scenario occurred at the beginning of the year, I knew nothing of Alfred's life or his aspirations. All I knew was that I wanted him to know that I welcomed him in my class and that I cared about more than just his knowledge and performance in mathematics. My question or comment to Alfred varied from day to day. Generally I asked him about the school and professional football games, how his previous weekend or evening was, his view on something that I had seen in the newspaper or on the television news, or whether he had difficulty with the homework assignment. I just wanted to engage him in a brief conversation.

Alfred was motivated to do mathematics because he believed that he could be successful.

After about two weeks of my talking with him before class, I was surprised that Alfred started to come to my class earlier and earlier. His behavior in class improved, and he actually started completing his homework assignments with some concern about how well he achieved. Certainly he was still playful in class, and we laughed a lot, but he no longer challenged me for the direction of class. More important was that Alfred began to learn algebra. He was motivated to do mathematics because he believed that he could be successful, and he knew that he would have my support when he had difficulty. With his new efforts I became aware that he was an average to above-average student in mathematics. Alfred became one of my successful students. He even requested to take geometry during the next school year.

As fate would have it, I was scheduled to teach geometry that next year and was to be Alfred's teacher. I was surprised when he told me later that he had made sure that he was signed up for my course. I had the privilege of teaching Alfred in three mathematics classes in three years. Certainly the years were not totally without challenges. I can remember many situations in which I had to pull him out of the classroom for private conversations because of his interactions with other students. But Alfred received the conversations with respect and with his understanding of my concern for his achievement and emotional development. The relationship that Alfred and I forged had transcended his constant need to disguise his lack of confidence through trying to exert power and control in class and had become one of mutual respect, reflecting his belief that he could be successful in mathematics. Alfred graduated from high school and was accepted into college. Our close relationship has lasted over the years and will last for our lifetime. This relationship and his understanding of mathematics were motivated, in part, by my asking him one question a day to let him know that I cared about him and his learning.

The strategy used in this instance demonstrates the power of a teacher's care and concern for a student. Even though the vignette described is from a high school class, the strategy presented can be used at any grade level. Here is a quote from a sixteen-year-old student who remembered his third-grade teacher as a motivating factor in his life (Burke 1996, p. 21):

> My third-grade teacher was the best. She made sure I learned. She taught me right from wrong. And she kept me out of trouble. She told me to be a leader, not a follower. And that's what I've done. She gave me pride and self-confidence. She made me understand what life is all about and how important it is to plan your life. Today I believe in myself. I'm never going to let her down.

Similarly as in my relationship with Alfred, the third-grade teacher described seems to have demonstrated care and concern for her student that stayed with him throughout his schooling. Just as displaying care can encourage change in students' reactions to learning and views of themselves, so appropriate classroom instructional strategies that focus on the specific needs of students can result in academic success in heterogeneous mathematics classrooms.

Instructional strategies that focus on the specific needs of students can result in academic success in heterogeneous mathematics classrooms.

Focus of This Three-Book Series

As we strive to provide students in classrooms from prekindergarten through grade twelve with opportunities to experience and learn mathematics that will serve them throughout their lifetimes, increasingly more teachers are presented with classrooms of students with a range of needs, backgrounds, expertise, and experience, including students who lack prerequisite skills and students who may be able to move forward quickly and with deep understanding. Recognizing that all classrooms are diverse, this NCTM series of three books (for grades Pre-K–5, 6–8, and 9–12) addresses instructional strategies that meet the needs of all students and offer them high-quality mathematics. The mathematical instructional strategies presented in these books reflect that diversity can come in the form of language, culture, race, gender, socioeconomic status, and ways of learning and thinking, as well as cognitive and emotional characteristics.

Diversity can come in the form of language, culture, race, gender, socioeconomic status, and ways of learning and thinking, as well as cognitive and emotional characteristics.

Guided by the vision of the NCTM *Principles and Standards for School Mathematics* (2000) document, which states, "Equity ... demands that reasonable and appropriate accommodations be made as needed to promote access and attainment for all students" (p. 12), these books are designed to help teachers meet the diverse needs of their students. The volumes focus on helping teachers determine *how* to support high-quality mathematics learning for diverse student populations in a given classroom. The articles in this volume are presented in one of three forms: (1) cases of classroom practice, (2) instructional strategies, and (3) teacher development.

- Case articles describe classroom practice that promotes the learning of all students. They offer rich descriptions of teachers' practice, students' activity, and students' resulting learning.
- Instructional-strategies articles offer glimpses of the implementation or impact of particular instructional practices that support mathematical learning, not only for one group of students but for students having many diverse needs. These articles give examples of instruction or mathematical tasks that are beneficial for all students but especially relevant to students not well served by traditional approaches.
- Teacher-development articles discuss important topics to help teachers develop their expertise in teaching students who have a range of needs, backgrounds, and experience.

We are pleased to offer articles that span the issues and recommendations for our practice in the education of all students in mathematics.

In this grades 6–8 volume of the Mathematics for Every Student series, we are pleased to offer articles that span the issues and recommendations for our practice in the education of all students in mathematics. A brief description of each of the articles in this book follows.

Synopses of Articles

Helping to frame the perspective driving this book series, which views all students as able to do mathematics, article 1, "Moving from Deficiencies to Possibilities" by Mark Ellis, raises questions about the traditional ways students in the United States have been labeled as proficient or not in school mathematics. In particular, he asks readers to consider the intent behind such concepts as "ability" and "differentiation," challenging us to think about creating possibilities for all students to succeed in mathematics.

In article 2, "Teachers' Questions and Their Impact on Students' Engagement and Learning," George Bright and Jeane Joyner ask teachers to consider the purpose behind the questions they pose in the classroom and the relationship this questioning has to students' learning. Specifically, they advocate and illustrate the use of three questioning strategies—*engaging, refocusing,* and *clarifying.*

In article 3, "What Question Would I Be Asking Myself in My Head? Helping All Students Reason Mathematically," Beth Herbel-Eisenmann and Mary Schleppegrell offer a specific instance of one teacher's deliberate use of communication strategies that serve to value students' mathematical thinking and challenge students to further refine their mathematical understandings. The authors' detailed examination of the classroom transcripts fosters insight into how those strategies can be implemented to great effect.

With a sneak peek into her classroom of learners who harbor doubts about their mathematical abilities, article 4, Crystal Hill's "Adding Integers: From the Classroom to the Field," demonstrates the power of embedding mathematics learning in meaningful contexts and giving students opportunities to engage in discussions focused on explaining and justifying mathematical procedures and relationships. By the time her students have completed the learning activities designed to build an understanding of integer operations, they find themselves taking ownership of mathematical knowledge they had once believed was inaccessible.

In article 5, “The Human Graph Project: Giving Students Mathematical Power through Differentiated Instruction,” David Pugalee, Adam Harbaugh, and Lan Quach offer another example of supporting students: learning by connecting real-life activities—in this instance making graphs outdoors with students serving as points—with mathematical concepts and relationships. Their article presents detailed discussion of both the lesson itself and how it can support meaningful learning for all students, in particular English language learners.

Sylvia Celedón-Pattichis, in article 6, “What Does That Mean? Drawing on Latino and Latina Students’ Language and Culture to Make Mathematical Meaning,” gives rich examples of instructional strategies that both build from, and build on, the knowledge and experiences that students bring to the mathematics classroom. These strategies can be generalized to any population of students as teachers consider the students in their own classrooms.

In article 7, “Self-Differentiating in Inclusion Classrooms: Opportunities to Learn,” Signe Kastberg, Wendy Otoupal-Hylton, and Sheri Farmer share the case of two learners who generate a mathematically rich, albeit divergent, solution to a problem involving area and perimeter. The authors’ discussion of the ways in which the students’ approach demonstrated mathematical understanding and the struggle of the teacher to recognize and value this thinking lead to a realization of the power of the students’ “self-differentiating” actions that allowed them to make sense of the mathematics.

In chapter 8, taking a more holistic perspective, Kristin Stang blends research and experience to offer strategies for “Supporting Middle School Students with Learning Disabilities in the Mathematics Classroom.” Her work focuses on accommodations that teachers can make to offer students with special needs equal access to mathematical knowledge.

Also drawing on research and classroom experience, Matt Jones, in article 9, offers instructional strategies that answer the question “My Students Aren’t Motivated; What Can I Do?” Following a brief overview of motivation theory, the author describes several strategies that teachers can implement immediately in their classrooms to help students form better connections with the mathematical content they are studying.

In the final article, “Approaches to Assessing Students’ Thinking from Analyzing Errors in Homework,” Shuhua An and Zhonghe Wu describe an efficient tool for managing homework that allows teachers to develop insights into students’ thinking across multiple levels of prior achievement. Their rich examples of teachers’ use of this tool demonstrate the power of this method and show how it can help teachers support all learners.

Carol E. Malloy
Series Editor

REFERENCES

Burke, Nancy. *Teachers Are Special.* New York: Random House, 1996.

Marquis, David M., and Robin Sachs. *I Am a Teacher: A Tribute to America's Teachers.* New York: Simon & Schuster, 1990.

McLeod, Douglas. "Research on Learning and Instruction in Mathematics: The Role of Affect." In *Integrating Research on Teaching and Learning Mathematics,* edited by Elizabeth Fennema, Thomas P. Carpenter, and Susan J. Lamon, pp. 55–82. Albany: State University of New York, 1991.

National Council of Teachers of Mathematics (NCTM). *Principles and Standards for School Mathematics.* Reston, Va.: NCTM, 2000.

1

Moving from Deficiencies to Possibilities: Some Thoughts on Differentiation in the Mathematics Classroom

Mark W. Ellis

What the learners conflict with in the mathematics classroom may not only be the mathematical meaning of a particular piece of content or a particular strategy, but the whole act of being taught through processes that ignore, reject or make invisible some students, processes destined to select a few and fail the rest.

—*Núria Gorgorió and Núria Planas*

KATHLEEN Collins's (2003) eighteen-month case study of Jay, a fifth-grade African American student, documents in detail the ways in which those in authority in his school "pathologized Jay's family structure, his cultural way of being" (p. 194) such that he was labeled as having low ability and was held to lower expectations by his teacher. Even after Collins shared samples of his work that clearly exhibited cognitive strengths, Jay's teacher "still responded to Jay as though he were less than capable" (p. xiii). The teacher's beliefs about Jay's abilities and, consequently, his academic needs were premised on a deficit model and reinforced by labels applied to him by the schooling process, leading her to discount evidence of his achievements as somehow immaterial. Although perhaps unintentional, the actions of his teacher served to limit the possibilities for Jay's success.

A practice exists in the United States of using school as a location in which to label students according to some perceived "ability" and separate them into different levels of coursework rather than see the potential for success that lies in every student (Oakes 2005). As this article's opening quote describes, this approach has led to practices in the mathematics classroom that often keep students from the mathematics rather than get them into it (Ellis 2007). Efforts to reform our teaching of mathematics such that a broader range of students have access to high standards and are supported in reaching those standards are often at odds with this practice or habit of mind. When thinking about the idea of differentiation in the mathematics classroom, how it is undertaken must be carefully considered—what are the assumptions and beliefs from which teachers work to differentiate instruction? This article is intended to stimulate readers to examine the positions from which their own efforts at differentiation are

When thinking about the idea of differentiation in the mathematics classroom, how it is undertaken must be carefully considered—what are the assumptions and beliefs from which teachers work to differentiate instruction?

enacted. Specifically, notions of ability are examined as social constructions that have a big impact on how efforts to differentiate instruction come to be crafted.

Since the early 1900s, school mathematics in the United States has offered a convenient location for the separation of students by so-called "ability" (Ellis 2008). Although concern about the overall mathematical knowledge of all students has become greater and greater in recent years (Diaz and Lord 2005; National Commission on Mathematics and Science Teaching for the Twenty-first Century 2000; National Council of Teachers of Mathematics [NCTM] 2000; U.S. Department of Education 2003), much of the energy being directed toward mathematics education remains focused on determining students' placement within a variety of leveled courses, planning and implementing separate curricula, and measuring the resulting variations in learning outcomes (Booher-Jennings 2005; Diamond and Spillane 2004). Although these efforts may be socially sought-after, they are in large part educationally counterproductive (Ayalon and Gamoran 2000; Boaler, Wiliam, and Brown 2000; Oakes 2005). As long as outcomes in mathematics achievement as measured by standardized examinations (and the resulting inferences about students' abilities in mathematics) continue to be correlated with such demographic markers as economic status, race, and ZIP code, the educational mission of schooling—that of supporting all students in reaching their full potential—has yet to be fulfilled.

At issue are conceptions of mathematical ability and students' potential and the impact that these factors have on teachers' decisions about how best to serve their students. Ample research has documented the ways in which poor academic performance among low-income and African American and Latino students is problematized such that students' characteristics and backgrounds are blamed, whereas such factors as opportunities to learn and access to information are ignored (Diversity in Mathematics Education Center for Learning and Teaching 2007; Oakes et al. 1997; Rubin 2008). Such deficit perspectives persist despite teachers' commonly stated belief that all students can succeed in school (Wilson and Corbett 2007).

Activating Students' Potential

Hearing talk about students who are of "low ability" or who "don't care" about learning or who "can't do math" leads me to think back to my experiences as a teacher of mathematics in low- to middle-income communities with students who were diverse not only ethnically, economically, and linguistically but also with respect to their existing knowledge of mathematics and their preferred learning modalities (e.g., visual, tactile). In my classroom students who did not care to do mathematics, who were not proficient in English, whose abilities in mathematics had been deemed to be low somehow found themselves learning mathematics. The cause of this apparent aberration was grounded in my refusal to base expectations for students' achievement on the labels applied to them by schools and society.

As a case in point, Alonso[1] was in my seventh-grade mathematics class along with twenty-four other students whose existing knowledge of mathematics was tenuous at best. The class average on their sixth-grade state mathematics examination placed them at the thirtieth percentile, far from what I considered their potential. Alonso's prior achievement in mathematics was well below that of his peers, in the single digits, a result that seemed inexorably linked with his being labeled as having low ability. Although I realized that he lacked *proficiency* with many mathematical concepts and skills, I did not equate this lack with Alonso's having a low *ability* to do mathematics. In fact, as I got to know Alonso, I learned that he had become accustomed to being left alone in class as long as he was not causing a distraction—left alone and not encouraged to learn to do mathematics (see Rousseau and Tate [2003] for research documenting how students from certain groups are "allowed to fail"). For me this neglect was at the root of his low achievement in mathematics.

Although I realized that he lacked proficiency with many mathematical concepts and skills, I did not equate this lack with Alonso's having a low ability to do mathematics.

Over the course of the two years that Alonso and his peers were in my mathematics class, through the seventh and eighth grades, they grew in every way imaginable—physically, socially, and, of course, academically. The class mean on the state mathematics examination increased to the sixty-third percentile, and Alonso's, to the sixty-fifth. Even more important, the students became doers of mathematics who communicated their thinking, challenged one another to justify strategies and outcomes, and strove to make sense of mathematics. This improvement took place in spite of the labels that had been applied to them by the schooling system and by society. These students' progress was made possible by my connecting mathematics with their lives through using contextualized problems; providing multiple pathways to learning important concepts, including the use of visual models; requiring them to achieve proficiency in prerequisite skills while at the same time engaging them in learning grade-level concepts; and holding them accountable for making progress that reflected their potential to make sense of mathematics. Their success was due to the phenomenal response by my students and their supportive families to the challenge to bring their proficiency in mathematics up to and above benchmarks set by the state standards.

Essential to this success was a perspective that a fundamental aspect of a teacher's job is to hold high expectations of every student's potential and to create possibilities for all students to learn in ways that respect who they are and recognize their strengths as learners. Bransford, Brown, and Cocking (2000, p. 6), in their landmark publication *How People Learn: Brain, Mind, Experience, and School*, state quite powerfully,

Essential to this success was a perspective that a fundamental aspect of a teacher's job is to hold high expectations of every student's potential and to create possibilities for all students to learn in ways that respect who they are and recognize their strengths as learners.

> Learning research suggests that there are new ways to introduce students to traditional subjects, such as mathematics, science, history and literature, and that these new approaches make it possible for the majority of individuals to develop a deep understanding of important subject matter.

1. This is a pseudonym.

This philosophy lies at the heart of efforts to make mathematics accessible to all students, a concept exemplified by the cases and strategies shared by the authors in this book. Rather than continue the legacy of separation and leveled expectations, teachers of mathematics must learn to recognize and teach to students' strengths.

Problematizing Differentiation

The *Oxford English Dictionary* (Simpson and Wiener 1989) defines *differentiate* as "To make or render different; to constitute the difference in or between; to distinguish." The term *differentiate* derives from *different,* meaning "not of the same kind; not alike; of other nature, form, or quality" (Simpson and Wiener 1989). The underlying concept in these terms is that of making comparisons with a standard or norm and recognizing objects that fall outside that norm. That "differentiate" came into common use in the mid- to late-1800s (Simpson and Wiener 1989) is indicative of Western imperialistic and rationalistic thought of an era in which dominant groups sought to bring under control those who were "other" than the norm (Willinsky 1998). Given this historical perspective, care must be taken when using a term such as *differentiation of instruction* if the aim is to give all students greater opportunity for meaningful learning to take place.

Indeed, when examining its use in education, one finds that differentiation of instruction is characterized in multiple and often discrepant ways. One well-known scholar of differentiation, Carol Tomlinson (2000, p. 1), contends, "Whenever a teacher reaches out to an individual or small group to vary his or her teaching in order to create the best learning experience possible, that teacher is differentiating instruction." The central idea in Tomlinson's depiction of differentiation is to *vary one's actions as a teacher to meet the needs of students.* Note that the focus here is on changing instructional practices, moving beyond the standard, or normative, habits that characterize mathematics teaching (e.g., teacher-led lecture and demonstration followed by individual students' work on rote procedures; see Stigler and Hiebert [1997]; Weiss et al. [2003]).

The central idea in Tomlinson's depiction of differentiation is to vary one's actions as a teacher to meet the needs of students.

In contrast with a focus on teachers' changing actions, Ayalon (2006) describes how differentiation is often viewed from a curricular perspective: "[A] differentiated curriculum enables students to enroll in courses that are congruent with their interests and abilities. The rationale behind level differentiation and formal tracking underscores the diversity in students' abilities and the need to offer programs that correspond to that diversity" (p. 1188). From this perspective, differentiation involves *changing the curriculum in response to students' perceived abilities.* Particularly in school mathematics, with its history of providing inequitable access to content on the basis of perceived ability, this latter take on differentiation is all too easily embraced—but should be vociferously avoided! Although teacher educators often frame differentiation much as Tomlinson does—as requiring teachers to respond to students' needs to make content accessible—in practice the curriculum is often changed because of perceived differences in students' abilities. I argue that the latter of these responses to differentiation is a consequence of the term itself that, together with a belief that mathematical ability is both accurately measurable and unevenly distributed, promotes actions that work against our efforts to create classroom environments in which all students learn meaningful mathematics.

Creating Possibilities for Students' Success

The challenge, then, is to move one's focus from "ability" to "possibility" by getting to know students' strengths and preferences among learning modalities, then implementing lessons that activate those strengths and build from existing knowledge. Meeting this challenge requires a new stance toward teaching mathematics that is premised on creating possibilities for students' learning, maintaining a perspective that expects students to be successful when provided access to important ideas, and furnishing support as students make sense of these ideas. This sort of differentiation, reflective of Tomlinson's definition, shifts teachers' attention away from activities that construct students as able or unable, directing attention instead toward strategies and situations that allow access for all students to learn mathematics. Too many "Jays" and "Alonsos" in our classrooms fall victim to traditional habits of teaching mathematics. Instead, our efforts to make content meaningful and accessible must activate the tremendous potential that lies within all students.

REFERENCES

Alayon, Hanna. "Nonhierarchical Curriculum Differentiation and Inequality in Achievement: A Different Story or More of the Same?" *Teachers College Record* 108, no. 8 (2006): 1186–1213.

Ayalon, Hanna, and Adam Gamoran. "Stratification in Academic Secondary Programs and Educational Inequality in Israel and the United States." *Comparative Education Review* 40 (2000): 54–79.

Boaler, Joan, Dylan Wiliam, and Margaret Brown. "Students' Experiences of Ability Grouping: Disaffection, Polarization, and the Construction of Failure." *British Educational Research Journal* 26, no 5 (2001): 631–48.

Booher-Jennings, Jennifer. "Below the Bubble: 'Educational Triage' and the Texas Accountability System." *American Educational Research Journal* 42, no. 2 (2005): 231–68.

Bransford, John D., Ann L. Brown, and Rodney R. Cocking. *How People Learn: Brain, Mind, Experience, and School.* Washington, D.C.: National Academies Press, 2000.

Collins, Kathleen M. *Ability Profiling and School Failure: One Child's Struggle to Be Seen as Competent.* Mahwah, N.J.: Lawrence Erlbaum Associates, 2003.

Diamond, John B., and James P. Spillane. "High-Stakes Accountability in Urban Elementary Schools: Challenging or Reproducing Inequality? *Teachers College Record* 106, no. 6 (2004): 1145–76.

Diaz, Alicia, and Joan Lord. *Focusing on Student Performance through Accountability.* Atlanta, Ga.: Southern Regional Education Board, 2005.

Diversity in Mathematics Education Center for Learning and Teaching. "Culture, Race, Power, and Mathematics Education." In *Second Handbook of Research on Mathematics Teaching and Learning,* edited by Frank Lester, Jr., pp. 405–33. Reston, Va.: National Council of Teachers of Mathematics, 2007.

Ellis, Mark W. "President's Choice: Constructing a Personal Understanding of Mathematics: Making the Pieces Fit." *Mathematics Teacher* 100, no. 8 (April 2007): 516–22.

———. "Leaving No Child Behind Yet Allowing None Too Far Ahead." *Teachers College Record* 110, no. 6 (2008): 1330–56.

Gorgorió, Núria, and Núria Planas. "Cultural Distance and Identities-in-Construction within the Multicultural Mathematics Classroom." *Zentralblatt für Didaktik der Mathematik* 37, no. 2 (2005): 64–71.

National Commission on Mathematics and Science Teaching for the Twenty-first Century. *Before It's Too Late.* Washington, D.C.: U. S. Department of Education, 2000.

National Council of Teachers of Mathematics. (NCTM). *Principles and Standards for School Mathematics.* Reston, Va.: NCTM, 2000.

Oakes, Jeannie. *Keeping Track: How Schools Structure Inequality.* 2nd ed. New Haven, Conn.: Yale University Press, 2005.

Oakes, Jeannie, Amy Stuart Wells, Makeba Jones, and Amanda Datnow, "Detracking: The Social Construction of Ability, Cultural Politics, and Resistance to Reform." *Teachers' College Record* 98, no. 3 (1997): 482–510.

Rousseau, Celia, and William F. Tate. "No Time Like the Present: Reflecting on Equity in School Mathematics." *Theory into Practice* 42, no. 3 (2003): 210–16.

Rubin, Beth H. "Detracking in Context: How Local Constructions of Ability Complicate Equity-Geared Reform." *Teachers College Record* 110, no. 3 (2008). Retrieved September 28, 2007, from www.tcrecord.org/Content.asp?ContentId=14603.

Simpson, John, and Edmund Weiner, eds. *Oxford English Dictionary.* 2nd ed. Broadbridge, Alderley, Wotton-under-Edge, Gloucestershire, England: Clarendon Press, 1989.

Stigler, James W., and James Hiebert. "Understanding and Improving Classroom Mathematics Instruction: An Overview of the TIMSS Video Study." *Phi Delta Kappan* 79, no. 1 (1997): 14–21.

Tomlinson, Carol. "Differentiation of Instruction in the Elementary Grades." *ERIC Digest* (August 2000). Document No. ED0-PS-00-7. Available at ericece.org.

United States Department of Education. (2003). "Proven Methods: The Facts about . . . Math Achievement." Retrieved October 7, 2003, from http://www.ed.gov/nclb/methods/math/math.pdf.

Weiss, Iris R., Joan D. Pasley, P. Sean Smith, Eric R. Banilower, and Daniel C. Heck. *Looking inside the Classroom: A Study of K–12 Mathematics and Science Education in the United States.* Chapel Hill, N.C.: Horizon Research, 2003. Retrieved August 15, 2006, from www.horizon-research.com/insidetheclassroom/reports/looking/.

Willinsky, John. *Learning to Divide the World: Education at Empire's End.* Minneapolis: University of Minnesota Press, 1998.

Wilson, Bruce, and Dick Corbett. "Students' Perspectives on Good Teaching: Implications for Adult Reform Behavior." In *International Handbook of Student Experience in Elementary and Secondary School,* edited by Dennis Theissen and Alison Cook-Sather, pp. 283–311. Dordrecht, Netherlands: Springer, 2007.

2

Teachers' Questions and Their Impact on Students' Engagement and Learning

George W. Bright
Jeane M. Joyner

TEACHERS have many reasons for asking questions during mathematics instruction. Thinking about important purposes for questions can help teachers refocus their instructional planning so that students learn more. Using different kinds of questions for different purposes can help differentiate instruction by tailoring instruction to the specific needs of students.

On the basis of data from observations of a national sample of 364 mathematics and science lessons in grades K–12, Weiss and her colleagues (2003) found that the most common instructional pattern is "low-level 'fill-in-the-blank' questions, asked in rapid-fire, staccato fashion, with an emphasis on getting the right answer and moving on, rather than helping the students make sense of the mathematics/science concepts" (p. 67). That is, instruction seems to be oriented much more toward covering the curriculum and getting students to say the right things instead of helping students make sense of the underlying mathematical ideas. Of course some exceptions were noted. Observers did find instances of lessons in which teachers were clearly using questions to assess what their students knew and simultaneously to help students think deeply about mathematics, but those instances were not common. Overall, however, "questioning is among the weakest elements of mathematics and science instruction, with only 16 percent of lessons nationally incorporating questioning that is likely to move student understanding forward" (p. 65).

Questioning Types and Purposes

Thinking differently about the purposes for questions has the potential of improving the quality of questioning and, as a result, the quality of instruction. In particular, we want to discuss three kinds of questions, described subsequently, that serve different purposes: (1) engaging questions, (2) refocusing questions, and (3) clarifying questions (Bright and Joyner 2004). The use of different kinds of questions can enhance the effectiveness of different components of instruction so that a greater percent of students

The use of different kinds of questions can enhance the effectiveness of different components of instruction so that a greater percent of students remain engaged in conversation about important mathematics ideas.

The work reported here was supported in part by grant number 9819914 from the National Science Foundation. The opinions expressed are those of the authors and do not necessarily reflect the position of the Foundation or any other government agency.

remain engaged in conversation about important mathematics ideas. Just as targeting questions to match different levels of understanding is a crucial element of serving the needs of different students, so thinking carefully about the purpose of asking a given question is a component of focused instruction.

Engaging questions invite students into a discussion, keep them engaged in conversation, invite them to share their work, or get answers "on the table." They are usually open-ended with multiple acceptable answers and are usually directed at the class as a whole. An engaging question is used at the start of a discussion, but it might also be used when students have begun to "tune out" during a discussion to bring the class back into conversation. For example, if the teacher has had multiple interchanges with one student about a particular solution, the rest of the students may need to be reengaged in the discussion. Engaging questions can help thread a discussion by involving many students in the conversation. If students fail to "tune in" to a class discussion or lose the sense of a discussion, they are not likely to remember the important mathematics ideas. Students who lack confidence in themselves as learners of mathematics might benefit most by being invited into discussions that reward multiple solutions based on alternative, correct mathematical reasoning.

Refocusing questions help students get back on track or move away from a dead-end strategy. Refocusing questions can, for example, remind students about some important part of a problem that they may be overlooking. Teachers often realize that students are going in the wrong direction, but simply telling them what to do differently may not be effective for long-term learning. Many times students are not ready to understand a teacher's thinking. Students need both to understand why a strategy is ineffective and to reorganize their thinking so that the same ineffective strategy is not used again. Telling them what to do differently, that is, simply substituting the teacher's thinking for students' thinking, is not likely to be effective for the purpose of helping students reorganize their thinking. Refocusing questions can also help keep a discussion from going off on a tangent; they can help to "cut off" an unproductive direction in a discussion.

Many times students are not ready to understand a teacher's thinking. Students need both to understand why a strategy is ineffective and to reorganize their thinking so that the same ineffective strategy is not used again.

Clarifying or probing questions help students explain their thinking or help the teacher understand their thinking. Clarifying questions can be used (a) when a teacher is fairly certain that students understand an idea but the language used to explain that thinking is not clear or precise or (b) when a teacher needs to reveal more about a student's thinking to make sense of it. In the first instance, clarifying questions help students make clear what is meant, both for themselves and for other students. Sometimes the request is as simple as asking students to specify the antecedent of a pronoun (e.g., What does "it" refer to?). In the second instance, clarifying questions become a crucial part of how a teacher comes to understand a student's thinking. A clarifying question used in this way can often expose a fundamental misunderstanding.

The most generic clarifying question, "How did you get that answer?" is often very useful at revealing two situations that may outwardly seem similar. One is that students understand an idea but do not communicate clearly about that understanding. For example, students may talk about the edges of a cube when they point to the faces of a cube. The other is that students truly misunderstand the mathematics but clearly communicate that misunderstanding. For example, students may incorrectly write $3\ 1/3 \times 4\ 1/5 = 12 + 1/15$. This distinction can be summarized by the phrase "miscommunicated understanding versus communicated misunderstanding."

Clarifying questions help students understand their thinking and self-check whether their contributions "fit" into a discussion. Asking a student to rephrase a comment allows the rest of the class a chance to think about what was said and to decide how their own thinking relates to that comment.

Clarifying questions can reveal the logic that students are using. This logic is likely to reflect both their academic backgrounds (that is, what they have previously learned) and their "real world" backgrounds (that is, what is happening in their lives outside school). The language that students use may give clues about what motivates them and what they see as an acceptable contribution in a discussion. For example, some students may live in home environments that encourage debate about decisions, whereas other students come from homes where adult authority is predominant. These differences may influence both the willingness of students to make contributions and the kinds of contributions that students are willing to make.

Sometimes teachers unintentionally exclude a group of students from meaningful participation through the kinds of questions they ask or the way that they phrase those questions. For example, beginning a discussion on reading graphs with the question "When you look at a graph in a magazine or newspaper, in what ways might that graph be misleading?" might put at a disadvantage those students who do not have access to magazines and newspapers at home.

Figure 2.1 shows a context that will help illustrate these three kinds of questions.

- *Engaging question*: How can we decide what value the question mark stands for?
- *Refocusing question*: What does it mean for two rectangles to be similar?
- *Clarifying question*: In response to a student who says that the answer is 5, How did you get 5?

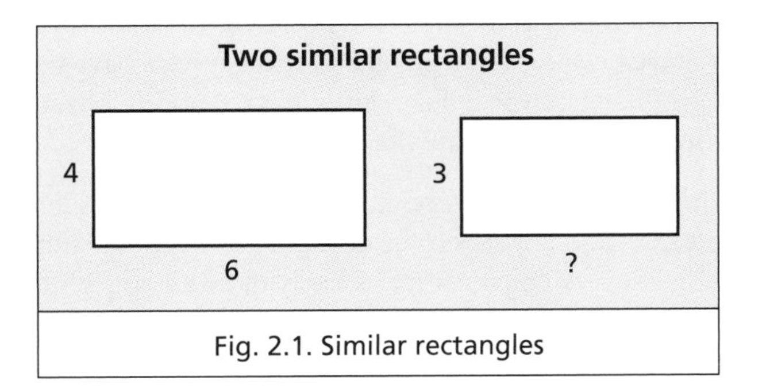

Fig. 2.1. Similar rectangles

Classifying questions according to a teacher's purpose provides a framework in which teachers can reflect on their reasons for asking particular questions. Reflection may lead to greater clarity of purpose as teachers plan instruction, and may help teachers avoid asking a series of low-level, short-answer questions that lead students through a specific strategy or lead students to say the answer without having to think seriously about the problem.

Suppose the learning target for a lesson is "distinguish area from perimeter." The underlying mathematics ideas are that perimeter is the distance around a plane figure and that area is a covering of the interior of a plane figure. An engaging question that might be used to initiate a discussion is "How would you go about finding the perimeter of the larger rectangle in figure 2.1?" This question encourages students to share a variety of strategies for finding perimeter: (a) Measure the sides and add. (b) Lay a string around the figure and then measure the string. (c) Put the figure on a grid, and hold it up to the window and count. An alternative engaging question is "How are perimeter and area different?" Students might respond in a variety of ways: (a) One you get by multiplying two sides, and the other you get by adding all four sides. (b) Perimeter is a length, and area is square units. (c) Perimeter is around the outside, and area is all the inside. By listening to different responses to an engaging question, a teacher can informally assess the understanding of the class.

Students often confuse perimeter and area, so refocusing questions might call attention to the differences in units that students use to record their answers. If a student says the area is 50 centimeters, a refocusing question might be "What kinds of units can you use to measure area?" This question calls attention generally to the difference in units for measuring perimeter and area. The student who says the area is 50 centimeters might also be asked a clarifying question, such as, "Why did you use centimeters to measure the area?" This question specifically targets the student's response rather than calls attention to a general mathematics idea.

Questions in a Classroom Context

One way to help teachers think about the purpose for questions is to have them analyze a conversation between a teacher and students.

One way to help teachers think about the purpose for questions is to have them analyze a conversation between a teacher and students. The particular example in figure 2.2 is based on a version of Fraction Tracks.

The conversation in figure 2.3 occurs when the teacher stops to talk with two students who have been playing the game. Although we cannot be absolutely certain of this teacher's purposes for the questions, most teachers who have been asked to engage in this exercise have reached consensus on the probable purpose for each of the questions. Discussing three of the questions can help illustrate the categories of questions.

- *How could you move your pieces across to the other side if our card was 8/10?* This question appears to be engaging. Indeed, the initial question in almost every conversation is likely to be an engaging question that invites students (in this situation, only two students) into the conversation. This question has multiple acceptable responses, and it may

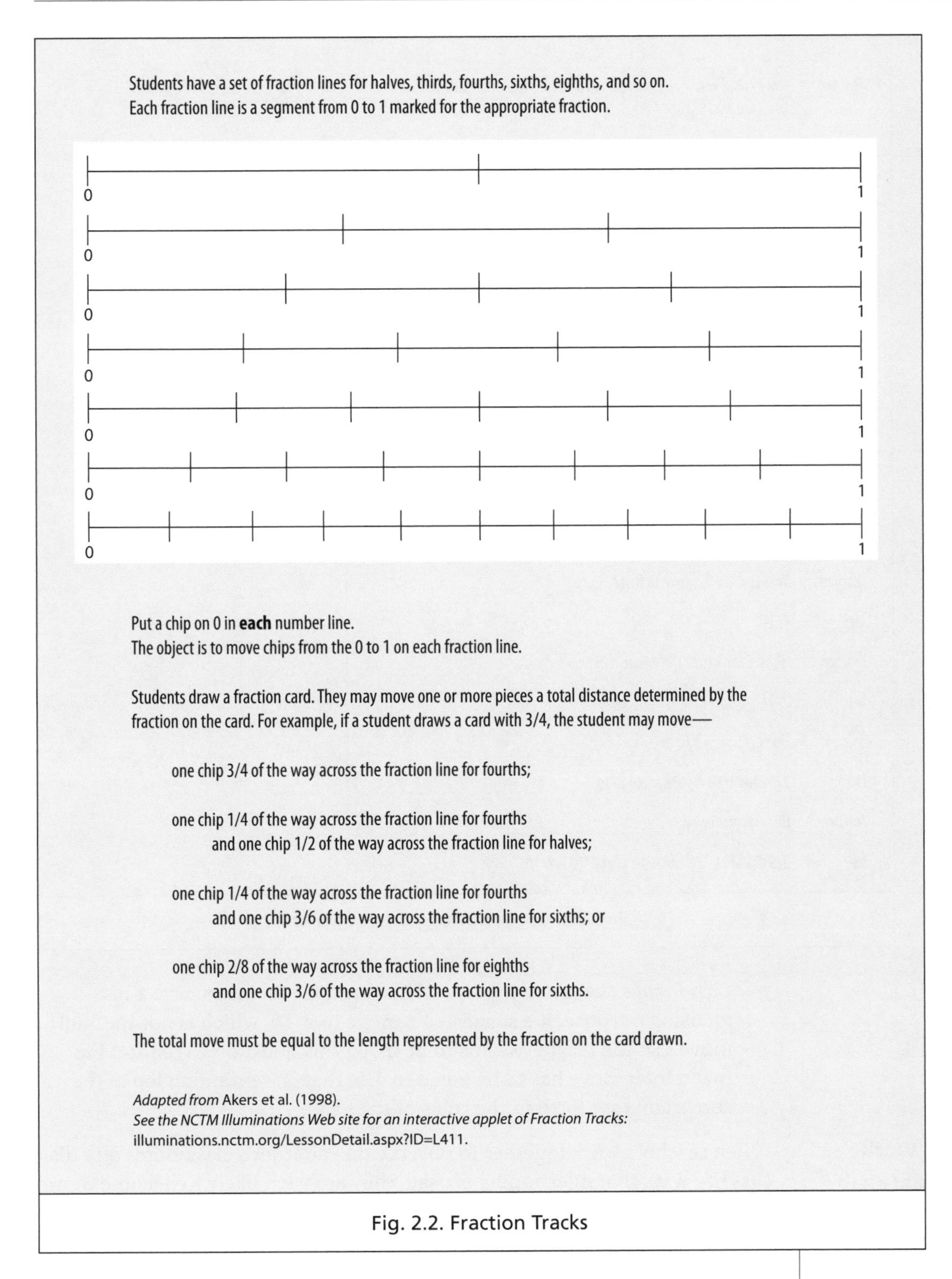

Fig. 2.2. Fraction Tracks

also have served the purpose of checking to learn how students interpreted the rules of the game.

- *Could you go 4/5 and then 8/10?* This question seems to be of a clarifying nature. Sue hesitated about the use of 8/10 and 4/5, so the teacher seems to be probing whether Sue is clear that the total for this move can be only 8/10 rather than 4/5 plus 8/10.

		Purpose of Question
Teacher:	How could you move your pieces across to the other side if our card was 8/10?	
Sue:	Instead of 8/10, you could use 2/5—no, 4/5—and you could go to 4/5 or 8/10.	
Teacher:	Could you go 4/5 and then go 8/10?	
Sue:	No. Only one of them.	
Teacher:	Why can you go 4/5?	
Sue:	Because 8/10 and 4/5 are the same. Both of them would work. Just use the row you need to finish.	
Teacher:	Is there a way I could move two pieces rather than one?	
Joe:	You can first go to 4/10. That would be half way, and then you can go to 4/5.	
Teacher:	Tell me how you're thinking about that.	
Joe:	They're both equivalent, so when you go half way ... (*hesitates*)	
Teacher:	Where did you move to first?	
Joe:	4/10.	
Teacher:	Okay. Can I move the whole 4/5 now?	
Joe:	2/5?	
Teacher:	Does 2/5 work?	
Joe:	2/5 plus 4/10 would equal 8/10.	
Teacher:	How do you know?	
Joe:	2/5 equals 4/10, and 4/10 plus 4/10 is 8/10.	

Fig. 2.3. Conversation with students

- *Can I move the whole 4/5 now?* This question seems to have a refocusing purpose. Joe suggested a move to 4/10, which is not the "full move"; so the teacher seems to be using this question to remind Joe that a total move has to be equal to 4/5, that is, reminding Joe of the constraints set forth in the rules of the game.

When teachers work together to observe one another's classrooms and discuss the ways that questioning is used, they are each likely to become more reflective about their own purposes for asking questions.

When teachers work together to observe one another's classrooms and discuss the ways that questioning is used, they are each likely to become more reflective about their own purposes for asking questions.

The teacher in the conversation seems to be probing the students' thinking about both the underlying mathematics and the context in which that mathematics is being used. Students need to understand the context of a problem, but because of the diversity of students in classrooms, teachers sometimes have difficulty finding contexts that "connect" with all students' backgrounds. Teachers may have to supply some "background information" about some contexts so that all students can make sense of those contexts.

This teacher also seems to be managing a conversation that engages both students. Students can learn to be flexible in their thinking by listening to their peers explain different approaches to a problem and then discussing those approaches to determine which ones are correct and efficient. Teachers can help students learn to respect the perspectives of their peers by respecting the perspectives of all students.

Questioning and Classroom Assessment

Teachers want to help students develop understanding of mathematics, and that outcome is most likely to happen when teachers have a clear sense of how students are thinking about mathematics. Classroom assessment, a type of formative assessment, is the process of gathering information about what students know and can do, making inferences from that evidence about students' mathematical understanding, and using those inferences to make instructional decisions that are aligned with the mathematical needs of the students. When classroom assessment is implemented effectively, it can change mathematics teaching and improve mathematics learning (Black et al. 2004; Black and Wiliam, 1998a, 1998b; Bright and Joyner, 2004–2005, 2006).

> Black and Wiliam (1998) conclude from an examination of 250 research studies on classroom assessment that "formative assessment does improve learning"—and that the achievement gains are "among the largest ever reported for educational interventions." The effect size of 0.7, on average, illustrates just how large these gains are.... In other words, if mathematics teachers were to focus their efforts on classroom assessment that is primarily formative in nature, students' learning gains would be impressive. These efforts would include gathering data through classroom questioning and discourse, using a variety of assessment tasks, and attending primarily to what students know and understand. (Wilson and Kenney 2003, p. 55)

When teachers' questions are successful at revealing students' mathematical understanding, instructional decisions can be made that better align instruction with students' needs. Suppose the teacher asks students what number goes in the box to make a true number sentence:

$$152 + 230 = \square + 240$$

Many middle-grades students will say, "382." If you ask them how they got their answer, the typical response is "I added 152 and 230," and some students will "finish" the problem by writing, "= 622" after 240. This response reveals a misunderstanding about the equals sign. Many students interpret the equals sign as indicating that an answer is to be written down rather than as indicating the need for "equating" or "equalizing" the values on either side of the equals sign. That is, the values on either side have to "balance."

In response to recognizing this fundamental misunderstanding, a teacher might organize a lesson around analyzing a variety of mathematically equivalent equations, such as the following:

How are these number sentences alike? How are they different?

$$152 + 230 = \square + 240$$

$$152 + 230 = 240 + \square$$

$$\square + 240 = 152 + 230$$

$$240 + \square = 152 + 230$$

How are these equations alike? How are they different?

$$241 + X = 376$$

$$241 + T = 376$$

$$241 + A = 376$$

For the first set of number sentences, students should come to realize that the answer is the same for all four number sentences. Because of the way the number sentences are written, students are likely to believe that 382 is *not* correct for the third example. This observation can lead to interesting discussions about why 382 is, therefore, also *not* correct for the first example. For the second set of equations, students should come to realize that the particular letter that is used for the missing value does not influence the missing value itself. These insights are important for preparing middle-grades students for algebraic reasoning.

Weiss and her colleagues (2003) suggest that a teacher's perception of what mathematics is important to learn is related to the kinds of questions asked.

> In many lessons mathematics and science are presented as static bodies of knowledge, focusing on vocabulary and algorithms. Observers of these lessons said things like "the teacher did the thinking throughout the lesson—there was no investigative spirit. The teacher had knowledge, which he attempted to transmit to students."... In a 9th-grade teacher's efforts to help his students better understand how to solve equations and inequalities, he asked them to remember and repeat the procedures he had demonstrated in the beginning of the class. The teacher's presentation of the content included questions and comments such as, "There's the variable, what's the opposite?" and "Tell me the steps to do." (p. 46)

Asking "better" questions has implications for the overall quality of instruction. "The vision of high-quality instruction should emphasize ... attention to appropriate questioning and helping students make sense of the mathematics/science concepts they are studying" (Weiss et al. 2003, pp. 104–5). Without knowledge of what students know and can do, helping students make sense of the mathematics they are learning is virtually impossible. Questions can help reveal what students know and understand, and in the process, students will learn to appreciate multiple perspectives on problems. Good questioning helps students become more flexible thinkers and be more comfortable with multiple ways of using important mathematics ideas.

REFERENCES

Akers, Joan, Cornelia Tierney, Claryce Evans, and Megan Murray. *Name That Portion: Fractions, Percents, and Decimals.* A unit of the Investigations in Number, Data, and Space curriculum. Parsippany, N.J.: Dale Seymour Publications, 1998.

Black, Paul, and Dylan Wiliam. "Assessment and Classroom Learning." *Assessment in Education* 5 (1998a): 7–74.

———. "Inside the Black Box: Raising Standards through Classroom Assessment." *Phi Delta Kappan* 80, no. 2 (1998b): 139–44.

Black, Paul, Christine Harrison, Clare Lee, Bethan Marshall, and Dylan Wiliam. "Working inside the Black Box: Assessment for Learning in the Classroom." *Phi Delta Kappan* 86, no. 1 (2004): 9–21.

Bright, George W., and Jeane M. Joyner. *Dynamic Classroom Assessment: Linking Mathematical Understanding to Instruction in Middle Grades and High School: Core Program: Facilitator's Guide.* Vernon Hills, Ill.: ETA/Cuisenaire, 2004.

———. "Classroom Assessment in Middle Grades and High School." *National Council of Supervisors of Mathematics Journal* 7, no. 2 (fall-winter 2004–2005), 11–17.

———. "Improving Mathematics Instruction through Formative Classroom Assessment. *New England Mathematics Journal* 38, no. 2 (2006): 23–35.

Weiss, Iris R., Joan D. Pasley, P. Sean Smith, Eric R. Banilower, and Dan J. Heck. *Looking inside the Classroom: A Study of K–12 Mathematics and Science Education in the United States.* Chapel Hill, N.C.: Horizon Research, 2003.

Wilson, Linda D., and Patricia A. Kenney. "Classroom and Large-Scale Assessment." In *A Research Companion to "Principles and Standards for School Mathematics,"* edited by Jeremy Kilpatrick, W. Gary Martin, and Deborah Schifter, pp. 53–67. Reston, Va.: National Council of Teachers of Mathematics, 2003.

3

"What Question Would I Be Asking Myself in My Head?" Helping All Students Reason Mathematically

Beth Herbel-Eisenmann
Mary Schleppegrell

A significant challenge in teaching mathematics is developing in students a sense of the intellectual significance of "doing math." Research on mathematics teaching and learning suggests that students need to learn to go beyond seeing mathematics as a set of procedures and instead learn to *reason* mathematically—to engage with mathematics as a thinking process rather than as a set of steps to move through in calculating a result to a problem.

Language use is crucial to accomplishing this goal because routines in language can influence what becomes normative (i.e., in roles, rights, responsibilities, and expectations) in the mathematics classroom (Herbel-Eisenmann 2000). Language use models ways of thinking about mathematics, so engaging students in reasoning mathematically enables them to adopt ways of "talking mathematics" that are valued by, and important to, the mathematical community. Developing norms for talking mathematics in valued ways in turn affects students' beliefs about mathematical activity (Cobb, Yackel, and Wood 1993), because classroom norms, language use, and students' beliefs are integrally related. When classroom language construes mathematics as a *process of reasoning*, students are engaged in learning mathematics in ways that define mathematical activity as more than a set of procedures to be followed, thus influencing their beliefs about what it means to know and do mathematics.

When classroom language construes mathematics as a *process of reasoning*, students are engaged in learning mathematics in ways that define mathematical activity as more than a set of procedures to be followed, thus influencing their beliefs about what it means to know and do mathematics.

As teachers, we cannot assume that all students come prepared to use language in school in the same way. As Schleppegrell (2004, pp. 21–22) points out,

> All children enter school with language resources that have served them well in learning at home and that have enabled them to be interactive and successful members of their families and local communities. But many children lack experience in making the kinds of meanings that are expected at

This article is based on work supported by the National Science Foundation (NSF) through grant number 0347906, Beth Herbel-Eisenmann, principal investigator. Any opinions, findings, conclusions, or recommendations expressed in this material are those of the authors and do not necessarily reflect the views of the NSF.

> school, or with the kinds of written texts and spoken interaction that prepare some children for school-based language tasks. This lack of experience makes it difficult for these students to learn and to demonstrate their learning.

We emphasize the fact that we are *not* saying that some students are deficient. Rather, we focus on the role of social experience in shaping what we know and can do, and we realize that some students' home experiences position them to respond more readily to traditional school discourses. In some homes, for example, children may be implicitly taught how to articulate an academic argument and may be encouraged to debate topics with one another and even with adults. In other homes, children may be told that they should not argue with one another or with adults because doing so is disrespectful. The children from homes where explanations are expected learn to draw on reasoned evidence when they argue, whereas children without such experience may tend to argue from their feelings. Clearly those children with experience making reasoned arguments are privileged by school discourses that value such reasoning; those without such experience need to develop new ways of arguing if they are to be successful in school. Thus, although all students come to school with discourse practices that serve them well in their homes and communities, some children need assistance in taking up the patterns of language that are valued in the school classroom. One of the teacher's responsibilities, then, is to use language in ways that explicitly demonstrate the kind of reasoning that is valued in different subjects to support all students' development of disciplinary thinking.

Language Moves in the Mathematics Classroom

In mathematics classrooms, teachers engage students in a variety of ways—for example, sometimes focusing on procedures, sometimes opening discussions about what students are doing and why they are doing it, and sometimes emphasizing big ideas and concepts. The NCTM clearly emphasizes this focus on both meaningful procedures and concepts in its *Principles and Standards for School Mathematics* (2000). Saenz-Ludlow and Walgamuth (2001) recommend that teachers of mathematics ask students to explain and justify answers, pose questions and problems to the class, and interpret the solutions of others, even disagreeing if the solution does not make sense. Teachers might also ask students to estimate answers, suggest alternative ways of finding answers, and evaluate the best operation to use to solve a problem, because this prompting gives the mathematical activity "an intellectual significance" (p. 29). As teachers engage in these *language moves*, however, they need to do so from an understanding of the underlying mathematics. For example, having students share solutions is important, but if teachers make explicit how two solutions are mathematically similar or different (especially if a solution is not appropriate), they can also coconstruct adequate *mathematical* explanations with students (Kazemi and Stipek 2001). We illustrate here language moves that show how teachers can consciously use language to develop students' mathematical thinking.

Mathematical reasoning does not come easily, and students need to hear the ways of explaining, justifying, and interpreting that are valued by the mathematical community. The teacher is well positioned to model these valued ways of talking and thinking about the principles that underlie the procedures. Teachers provide such modeling by explicitly drawing students' attention to the practices they are engaged in during mathematical activities—naming, explaining, and possibly even critiquing these practices.

Mathematical reasoning does not come easily, and students need to hear the ways of explaining, justifying, and interpreting that are valued by the mathematical community.

Researchers have described the different ways that teachers model such reasoning, calling more explicit language moves that include reflection on mathematical actions "stepping out" (Rittenhouse 1998) or "talking about talking about mathematics" (Cobb, Yackel, and Wood 1993). While solving a problem, a teacher might stop to comment on the mathematical process more explicitly, saying, for example, "That's a great example of the kind of explanation I'm looking for. It's important that you not only give your answer but that you also explain *what* you did and *why* you did it. I want you to explain the process you went through, not just give an answer." In this statement, the teacher is not just talking about the problem at hand; rather, she is "stepping out" of the discussion of the problem's solution to explicitly state her expectations for an appropriate mathematical explanation.

A less explicit way of drawing students' attention to the practices they are engaged in is "revoicing" (O'Connor and Michaels 1993, 1996), a language move that allows the teacher to reformulate a student's response by clarifying or extending what a student has said in an effort to help other students understand the mathematical significance of the contribution. Examples of revoicing include a teacher's recasting of a student's contribution in more technical terminology and "advance[ing] her own agenda, changing the contribution slightly so as to drive the discussion in another direction" (O'Connor and Michaels 1996, p. 74–75). Teachers use revoicing to clarify statements, make connections, or fill in missing elements of an explanation. By helping students articulate their understanding, teachers provide opportunities for students to agree or disagree with the reformulated version, teaching them to explain their reasoning.

By helping students articulate their understanding, teachers provide opportunities for students to agree or disagree with the reformulated version, teaching them to explain their reasoning.

Adler (1999) has shown that the issue of making language transparent—either by stepping out of the practice to comment on it or by revoicing students' comments—is complex, especially in settings where teachers work with students from different linguistic and cultural backgrounds. She points out that helping students learn appropriate ways of talking about mathematics without overwhelming them with teacher talk is not always an easy task (Adler 1997, 1998). Even though revoicing is teacher talk, it is talk that shows that a student's contribution is valued, and by extending a student's contribution, it can encourage further attempts by students to engage in mathematical reasoning.

In this article, we draw on data from one eighth-grade mathematics class to illustrate some of the ways the teacher used the language moves of stepping out and revoicing to make mathematical content and processes more explicit to students, moving from *doing* to *reflecting* in systematic ways. We begin by providing background information about the teacher, Jackie, and the mathematical context. We then present examples from her classroom practice that illustrate the language moves she uses to make mathematical content, language, and processes more explicit to students. The teacher models the kinds of questions the students should be considering, "steps out" to reframe the issues under discussion or extend them to other contexts, and asks students to use language to articulate principles. She also adopts a less explicit approach through her use of revoicing to validate and evaluate the ways students express their thinking, providing opportunities for them to recognize valued ways of construing mathematics in language. Such practices help all the students in the class further their mathematical understanding. We suggest that this teacher's practice illustrates how effective use of language and a push to engage students in language use enrich the mathematics classroom by making the ways of thinking that underlie mathematics available to all students.

Background

Jackie has taught middle-grades mathematics for about fifteen years and is a leader in her school and the broader mathematics education community. She was involved in pilot testing middle school mathematics curriculum materials funded by the National Science Foundation, *Mathematics in Context* (National Center for Research in Mathematics and Science Education and Freudenthal Institute 1997–98). These curriculum materials go beyond a focus on skills to introduce and develop mathematical ideas through the use of problem-solving contexts. An award-winning teacher who is involved in professional organizations (e.g., NCTM, NCSM) and professional development opportunities, Jackie recently became involved in a project that focuses on classroom discourse, allowing us to identify how she provides opportunities for students to reason mathematically. This article draws on data from that project, analyzing videotaped episodes that highlight Jackie's use of language and her efforts to move students beyond procedural explanations to more engagement with the mathematical concepts that underlie the procedures. Additionally, we have had conversations with Jackie about her classroom practices that offer insights into her pedagogical decisions.

As we observed and analyzed Jackie's teaching of many different mathematical topics during the 2005–2006 school year, we became aware of her consistent use of language to engage students in going beyond procedural knowledge about mathematics. In this article, we show how she uses the topic of *dividing fractions* to draw students' attention to the mathematical reasoning underlying this procedure. According to Jackie, when students get to her eighth-grade class, they often know the rule that to divide fractions you "invert and multiply." But Jackie wants the students to know more than this memorized procedure and to think about what they are actually doing when they invert and multiply. Early in the school year, Jackie prepares activities that engage students in making sense of what they are doing when they divide fractions, so they come to understand the relationship between multiplication and division of fractions. She starts with division of whole numbers and asks them, for example, what 24 divided by 8 *means*. Her point is to focus students' thinking on the underlying question that they are trying to answer by solving the problem. Students usually reply that it means "How many 8s are there in 24?" Jackie connects this idea with fraction problems, for example, 3/4 divided by 1/4, by asking, "How many one-fourths are in 3/4?"

Furthermore, Jackie has students examine sets of equations like those given in table 3.1 so that they can see that dividing by a number is the same as multiplying by that number's reciprocal. Typically, she presents each set of equations separately and then asks students, "What's the same and what's different between these two sets of equations?" Students usually observe that the first number, equals sign, and answer remain the same and that the division sign and second number change. Finally, students' attention becomes focused on the fact that the second number in the multiplication problem is the reciprocal of the second number in the division problem. This observation spurs a longer exploration to test more equations to see if this relationship is true for other problems.

Table 3.1
Dividing by a Number Is the Same as Multiplying by Its Reciprocal

Dividing by a Number	Multiplying by the Number's Reciprocal
16 / 4 = 4	16 × 1/4 = 4
20 / 10 = 2	20 × 1/10 = 2
12 / 3 = 4	12 × 1/3 = 4
15 / 5 = 3	15 × 1/5 = 3

We focus here in detail on activities related to dividing fractions that became part of the warm-up problems Jackie often did at the beginning of the class, prior to the *Mathematics in Context* explorations. Over the week of instruction from which this analysis is drawn, Jackie consistently required students to move beyond the "invert and multiply" mantra and helped them think about the reasoning behind the algorithm; see table 3.2 for a summary of the ways she did so. In the next section, we illustrate how Jackie's language moves make mathematical reasoning a focus of attention for her students. Throughout each example, we italicize instances of language moves—stepping out and revoicing—that are important to students' learning, and we discuss those moves following each example. The teacher's use of stepping out and revoicing consistently positions students as thinkers and explainers of mathematics, sending the message that mathematics allows for multiple solutions and calls for certain ways of reasoning and explaining. We summarize these roles and positions in our discussion of the examples.

The teacher's use of stepping out and revoicing consistently positions students as thinkers and explainers of mathematics, sending the message that mathematics allows for multiple solutions and calls for certain ways of reasoning and explaining.

Table 3.2
Jackie's Important Language Moves

Language Moves	Purposes for the Language Moves	Examples from the Transcript
• Bridging from what they did to what they were thinking	Linking action with reflection	• *... in my head...* • *... that's what you were thinking?* • *Moving from How would I write that out ...? to Why is that true?* • *What did you do and why?* • *... tell me what you think about when you see a question like that first one.* • *So, what did you think about when you did this one?*
• Modeling mathematical questions to ask yourself • Requesting reasons for answers • Focusing on making sense and understanding	Asking students to articulate the meaning behind the procedure	• *What question would I be asking myself in my head as I start that problem? What question is this problem asking? What are you thinking to yourself that this problem is asking?* • *Why is that true?* • *Does that [Tammy's explanation] make sense?* • *But they want to know why, they want to understand.* • *If I were going to estimate, what would I do to estimate the answer here?* • *How can you explain that to a sixth grader?*
• Stepping out to give students an audience to explain to • Requesting, naming, and validating multiple solutions • Revoicing to amplify and refine • Evaluating students' explanations	Defining what are "valued" explanations in mathematics	• *So you simplified this, changed it back to a mixed number and simplified?* • *So there's a couple of different ways people thought about this. One was just reasoning through it, one was just dividing by the coefficient of y, and one was thinking, What do I need to do to get one y? ... some different strategies, but they all got the same answer...* • *[revoices Tammy's solution]* • *Segueing from Monica's divided by one-third to divided both sides by one-third* • *"Just is" isn't a good explanation that helps me understand.*

Examples of Jackie's Language Moves

A few minutes into the class period, Jackie told students that she had put some problems on the board that she wanted them to work on (see fig. 3.1). As students worked at their desks, Jackie moved around the room to assess students' work informally, answer questions, and ask students to explain their thinking.

1.	Solve $x - 7 = 15x + 21$.
2.	Compute $4 \div 1/2 =$ _____.
3a.	I have *c* coins. One-fourth are dimes. How can I represent the <u>number</u> of dimes?
3b.	How can I represent the <u>value</u> of those dimes?

Fig. 3.1. Warm-up problems, Day 1 observation

Jackie then proceeded to work through the problems with the whole class. The second problem,

$$4 \div \frac{1}{2},$$

provided an opportunity for students to talk about the division of fractions.

001 Jackie: ... Now, #2. I'm doing a division problem, *so what question would I be*
002 *asking myself in my head as I start that problem?* Tammy.
003 Tammy: How many halves in four?
004 Jackie: How many halves are in four? Okay, and when I ask that question, it is
005 pretty obvious what the answer is. How many?
006 Students: Eight.
007 Jackie: Eight. Okay. *What if I'm going to write my intermediate step? How would*
008 *I write that out?* Sachin, what would I write out here? Four divided by a half is
009 the same as ...
010 Sachin: Times two
011 Jackie: Times two. And I get eight ... *Why is that true?* Sandy.
012 Sandy: Because with fractions dividing by a fraction is the same as multiplying
013 by a reciprocal.
014 Jackie: Okay, good. Now, *yesterday, a sixth-grade teacher asked me how do I*
015 *explain to my students why that's true. We know that there is a procedure, but*
016 *why is it true that dividing by a reciprocal is the same as multiplying by,* [that is]
017 *dividing by a fraction is the same as multiplying by the reciprocal? How can you*
018 *explain that to a sixth grader so they would understand why that's true?* Does
019 anybody have any suggestions for that teacher? Raise your hand if you have an
020 idea.
021 Kelly: It just is.

022 Jackie: *"Just is" isn't a good explanation. And "just is" is not an explanation*
023 *that helps me understand.* (laughs) Huh?
024 Ms: (inaudible)
025 Jackie: What's the sixth grader? But *they want to know why, they want to*
026 *understand.* Alisa, do you have a suggestion?
027 Alisa: For that problem, there's two halves in every one, because four wholes, so
028 multiply four by two.
029 Jackie: *So you can relate it to a particular instance where it can make sense in*
030 *that particular problem.* Okay? *Think about if you have any other suggestions*
031 *because it's kind of a hard question,* and that's what teachers have to think about.
032 Kelly: Is this like a real person?
033 Jackie: Yes, this is a true, true story. No, I'm not making it up. True story. That's
034 what I've been thinking about what, so *I had some ideas like you did. Take*
035 *somewhere we can see the answer pretty easily and work from there. But I didn't*
036 *have a really good answer to that, that I was really happy with. So, that's why*
037 *I'm asking you. So if you think of something, let me know.* Okay. Yeah, Carl?
038 Carl: Is it divided by half and since multiplication is opposite, can do opposite
039 with the opposite.
040 Jackie: Okay, *that's another way you can think about it. You kind of do the opposite of opposite, so it's the same* (laugh). Okay, that's true.

In this interaction, we see Jackie engaged in strategies that foreground students' mathematical reasoning. Her language moves are purposeful in *linking action with reflection, asking students to articulate the meaning behind the procedures, and defining what is valued in mathematical explanations.* Let us look at how she does so.

Lines 001–002 are typical of the way Jackie links action with reflection. In asking, *What question would I be asking myself in my head as I start that problem?* she communicates to students the fact that she is not just interested in the right answer; she wants them to think about the underlying principles and the meaning of the problem before they begin to solve it. Students are prepared to respond to such a request, as we see in Tammy's answer (line 003). Jackie extends Tammy's response by acknowledging that students would easily be able to answer the question that Tammy has asked (*it is pretty obvious*). The choral response of the students confirms how obvious it is! Jackie goes on to engage the students in further interaction that moves from procedure to reflection on it (line 007: *How would I write that out?...*; line 011: *Why is that true?*) Throughout the transcripts of Jackie's interaction with the students, we see that she regularly follows her requests for procedures with requests for *why* the procedure is being used. Linking action with reflection is important because it offers a means of moving students from the more everyday way of talking about mathematics (what we are *doing*), to a more academic or mathematical way of talking that engages students in thinking about *why* the process works the way it does.

Jackie "steps out" of the discussion to ask students to articulate the reasons behind the procedures, pushing the students to even more abstract reasoning when she asks them to help her explain why multiplying by a reciprocal is the same as dividing by a fraction. This episode, lines 014–040, illustrates how difficult it is for students to conceptualize mathematics in this way. Jackie helps them see what is valued in mathematical explanations by responding to each attempt by a student, first by rejecting a nonexplanation (021) and then by pointing out that another explanation is giving a *particular* example rather than explaining the process in a general sense (028). She even admits that using a particular example is the strategy she thought of (033), but that she was not "really happy" with that (035). This comment pushes Carl to a more general, abstract explanation (037), which the teacher takes up briefly before moving on to the next problem.

Throughout the transcripts of Jackie's engagement with students about understanding dividing fractions, a significant move that she often makes is to ask, *What question is this problem asking?* She often asks students to estimate, even when estimation is not called for in the problem, thus helping students develop flexibility in understanding what a reasonable answer might be. Her *restating* and *revoicing* are pervasive moves that she employs to focus students' attention on the relationships rather than procedures, making the language for describing the processes more precise as well. We see this approach in another excerpt from classroom dialogue two days after the example above, when the class was discussing another warm-up problem,

$$\text{Solve for } y\text{: } \frac{1}{3}y = 12\text{:}$$

041 Jackie: ... Evan, can you *tell me what you think about* when you see a question
042 like the first one.
043 Evan: Can I read? It's one-third of y equals twelve.
044 Jackie: Okay, one-third of y equals twelve. If *you read it that way*, it helps you
045 right there. So *what did you think about* when you did this one?
046 Evan: Um, I thought that the twelve is, whatever. Like whatever one-third y is,
047 it's twelve, so I just went and did like twelve times two—twelve times three—
048 and I got thirty-six.
049 Jackie: Okay.
050 Evan: And twelve is [inaudible]
051 Jackie: Okay, *and you can check your answer because one-third of thirty-six is*
052 *twelve.* Okay? Monica, *when you did it, what were you thinking*? You were
053 *thinking a little differently* [than Evan]. What did you think about to solve this?
054 Monica: Um, I just, um, divided by one-third.
055 Jackie: Divided *both sides* by one-third. What's one-third divided by one-third?
056 One, right? Something divided by itself. When I divide twelve by one-third,
057 *dividing by a fraction is the same as multiplying by its reciprocal.* So twelve
058 times three would give me thirty-six. Sandy, what did you think about when you
059 did it? ...
060 Sandy: I did times three on both sides.

061	Jackie: Okay. *Because three times a third is?* ...
062	Sandy: Oh, one.
063	Jackie: One. Okay. *So one y is what we want,* and so twelve times three gives us the
064	thirty-six. *So there's a couple of different ways people thought about this.*
065	*One was just reasoning* through it, *one was just dividing by the coefficient* of *y*,
066	and *one was thinking, What do I need to do to get one y*? Multiply by three. Okay, so
067	you had *some different strategies, but they all got you the same answer,* which is a
068	good thing. And *we checked that that answer worked because* a third of thirty-six
069	is twelve.

Jackie asks Evan to use language to express the mathematical symbolism at 044–045. Evan focuses on the procedure (*I went and did....*), and after reminding the students about the procedure for checking their answers (051), Jackie once again focuses the students' attention on *what were you thinking* and not *what did you do* at 052–053. Monica stays with *what she did,* but Jackie uses that comment to bring up the generalization again about the relationship between the reciprocal and the fraction. Jackie asks students to extend their understanding of the meaning of division of fractions (*dividing by a fraction is the same as multiplying by its reciprocal,* 057) by considering a new context, helping students see that this relationship remains consistent even when solving equations. She recasts the students' contributions at the end of this excerpt (063–067), naming their strategies with more precise language than they used, enabling them to gain experience with how to reason mathematically.

Language Use, Classroom Norms, and Students' Beliefs

In the examples from Jackie's classroom, her language moves define her role in the classroom as someone who requests multiple solutions, amplifies students' solutions, revoices students' contributions to make them more mathematically clear and precise, makes students aware of mathematical thinking and relationships, and helps students develop ways of thinking and talking about mathematics as a reasoning process. In turn, these language moves position the students as people who are mathematical thinkers, solution generators, and explainers. These student-roles characterize the students as being mathematically competent and not just following procedures that have been defined without meaning. Furthermore, because these language moves are a regular feature of Jackie's teaching, she sends the message to students that mathematics is flexible, makes sense, has meaning, requires reasons for its procedures, and requires particular kinds of explanations.

This careful attention to language moves in mathematics classrooms gives all students opportunities to engage in mathematical reasoning. Students with fewer opportunities for academic language development outside the classroom need repeated experiences and engagement with the ways of interacting about mathematics that are valued at school. For example, in their investigation of a secondary school precalculus class in which the teacher expected technical language from students and had them talk a lot about mathematical ideas, Huang, Normandia, and Greer (2005) found that even with practice, students had difficulty taking up the teacher's ways of mathematical reasoning. They suggest that students need explicit instruction in articulating principles and not just focusing on the description, sequence, and choice that are practical aspects of mathematical knowledge. In our own data, Jackie's language moves represent the kind of modeling that shows students how to be effective participants in mathematical discourse. Her requests for students to articulate their thinking processes help all students learn about appropriate mathematical explanations and meanings, and her stepping out and revoicing make accessible to students the thinking Jackie is engaging in as she works through mathematics problems. Figure 3.2 shows how these language moves are tied to the classroom norms that Jackie develops and the messages about mathematics that are reflected in her discursive practices.

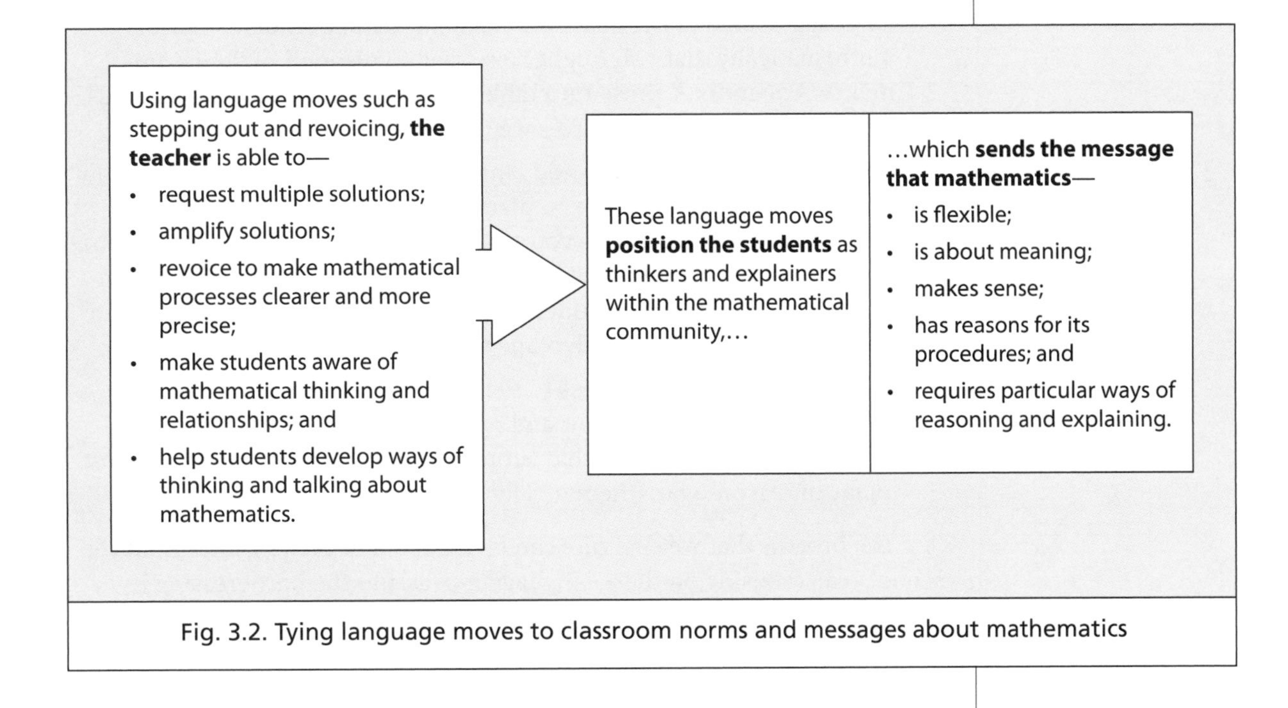

Fig. 3.2. Tying language moves to classroom norms and messages about mathematics

Investigating Your Language Moves in the Classroom

Developing reasoning about mathematics takes time, and teachers at all levels can help students begin to do so by modeling ways to talk about mathematics, reasoning about the activities they are engaged in, and responding to students' contributions in ways that extend and support their development of academic language. We suggest trying the language moves of stepping out and revoicing in your own classroom and examining the ef-

Developing reasoning about mathematics takes time, and teachers at all levels can help students begin to do so by modeling ways to talk about mathematics, reasoning about the activities they are engaged in, and responding to students' contributions in ways that extend and support their development of academic language.

fect these moves have on your students. Action research[1] is a powerful way for teachers to investigate what happens when new ways of interacting are introduced. Action research can help you identify and assess the language moves you make as you try to push students toward more mathematical ways of reasoning. The following process can be used to record and reflect on your classroom interactions:

- Select a focus day, and use an audio or video recorder to capture the conversation that takes place. Teachers who do action research on their classroom discourse highlight the importance of listening to themselves in their classroom. (See, for example, Ballenger [1999]; Gallas [1995].)
- Afterward, listen to the recorded interaction, attending carefully to the language moves you make, in particular focusing on the ways you ask students to link action with reflection, articulate the meaning behind a procedure, and respond to students' explanations. Identify what you like about the moves you make as well as instances where you may have been able to use these moves more effectively. Think of specific language related to the goals you have for helping students reason mathematically that you might have used to respond to their comments. Appendix A presents a table that can be used to focus your attention on the language moves we describe in this article.
- Select another focus day to add language moves or change some of the ways you use language. As you plan your lesson, try to anticipate the multiple solution strategies your students might offer and identify potential sources of confusion. Use that information to decide what language moves might help students focus on reasoning, explaining, and reflecting. Audiotape or videotape the lesson again on this focus day.
- Repeat the reflection process to examine your language moves until you believe that stepping out and revoicing have become integrated into your practice in ways that support students' use of academic language in reasoning mathematically.

The process that we describe can be repeated in cycles throughout the school year, focusing on these language moves and then progressing to others. (See, for example, Chapin, O'Connor, and Anderson [2003] for additional suggestions of language moves mathematics teachers might consider.) Reasoning mathematically is essential to every goal of mathematics education. Planning for classroom interaction is a way to offer all students opportunities to observe mathematical reasoning in action and to develop their own abilities with mathematical reasoning. Attending to language moves in the classroom that both reveal your own thinking processes and clarify those of your students is a step toward constructing more meaningful mathematics learning for all students, particularly those for whom such patterns of interaction may not be familiar.

---

1. NCTM has recently released a set of books that highlight rich examples of mathematics teachers involved in action research (e.g., Masingila [2006] and Van Zoest [2006]). Many of the articles in these volumes are related to language and discourse or have an emphasis on social justice.

APPENDIX A
Identifying Your Language Moves

This form can be used to document your language moves as you listen to the recording of your lesson. When you hear yourself making one of these moves, note where it occurs, how students respond, and how you follow up. Then listen again, trying to identify other moments in the lesson when you could have used a language move that might have supported students' development of mathematical reasoning and understanding.

Language Moves	**When It Occurs** (Note what is happening in the lesson at this moment.)	**How Students Respond and How You Followed Up** (Write down the exact words you and the students use so you can think about the kind of mathematical knowledge development that you have supported.)
Moving from what students ***did*** to what they were ***thinking*** How to identify: *Listen for times when students say what they are doing and you ask them about their thinking.*		
Asking students to articulate the meaning behind the procedure How to identify: *Listen for times when you ask students to give reasons for their answers or to explain what they are doing or thinking.*		
Defining "valued" explanations in mathematics How to identify: *Listen for times when you "revoice" a student's wording, ask students to explain in a different way, give reasons why an explanation is effective, or ask for multiple solutions.*		

REFERENCES

Adler, Jill. "A Participatory-Inquiry Approach and the Mediation of Mathematical Knowledge in a Multilingual Classroom." *Educational Studies in Mathematics* 33 (1997): 235–58.

———. "A Language of Teaching Dilemmas: Unlocking the Complex Multilingual Secondary Mathematics Classroom." *For the Learning of Mathematics* 18, no. 1 (1998): 24–33.

———. "The Dilemma of Transparency: Seeing and Seeing through Talk in the Mathematics Classroom." *Journal for Research in Mathematics Education* 30, no. 1 (January 1999): 47–64.

Ballenger, Cynthia. *Teaching Other People's Children: Literacy and Learning in a Bilingual Classroom.* New York: Teachers College Press, 1999.

Chapin, Suzanne H., Mary C. O'Connor, and Nancy C. Anderson. *Classroom Discussions: Using Math Talk to Help Students Learn.* Sausalito, Calif.: Math Solutions Publications, 2003.

Cobb, Paul, Erna Yackel, and Terry Wood. "Theoretical Orientation." In *Rethinking Elementary School Mathematics: Insights and Issues, Journal for Research in Mathematics Education* Monograph No. 6, edited by Terry Wood, Paul Cobb, Erna Yackel, and Deborah Dillon, pp. 21–32. Reston, Va: National Council of Teachers of Mathematics, 1993.

Cochran-Smith, Marilyn. "Series Forward." In *Teachers Engaged in Research: Inquiry into Mathematics Classrooms, Grades 6–8,* edited by Joanna O. Masingila. Greenwich, Conn.: Information Age Publishing, 2006. Available from the National Council of Teachers of Mathematics.

Gallas, Karen. *Talking Their Way into Science: Hearing Children's Questions and Theories, Responding with Curricula.* New York: Teachers College Press, 1995.

Herbel-Eisenmann, Beth A. "How Discourse Structures Norms: A Tale of Two Middle School Mathematics Classrooms." Doctoral dissertation, Michigan State University, East Lansing, Mich., 2000.

Huang, Jingzi, Bruce Normandia, and Sandra Greer. "Communicating Mathematically: Comparison of Knowledge Structures in Teacher and Student Discourse in a Secondary Math Classroom." *Communication Education* 54, no.1 (2005): 34–51.

Kazemi, Elham, and Deborah Stipek. "Promoting Conceptual Thinking in Four Upper-Elementary Mathematics Classrooms." *Elementary School Journal* 102, no. 1 (2001): 59–80.

Masingila, Joanna O., ed. *Teachers Engaged in Research: Inquiry into Mathematics Classrooms,Grades 6–8.* Greenwich, Conn.: Information Age Publishing, 2006. Available from the National Council of Teachers of Mathematics.

National Center for Research in Mathematics and Science Education and Freudenthal Institute. *Mathematics in Context: A Connected Curriculum for Grades 5–8.* Chicago: Encyclopaedia Britannica Educational Corporation, 1997–98.

National Council of Teachers of Mathematics (NCTM). *Principles and Standards for School Mathematics.* Reston, Va.: NCTM, 2000.

O'Connor, Mary Catherine, and Sarah Michaels. "Aligning Academic Task and Participation Status through Revoicing: Analysis of a Classroom Discourse Strategy." *Anthropology and Education Quarterly* 24 (1993): 318–35.

———. "Shifting Participant Frameworks: Orchestrating Thinking Practices in Group Discussion." In *Discourse, Learning, and Schooling,* edited by Deborah Hicks. New York: Cambridge University Press, 1996.

Rittenhouse, Peggy S. "The Teacher's Role in Mathematical Conversation: Stepping In and Stepping Out." In *Talking Mathematics in School: Studies of Teaching and Learning*, edited by Magdelene Lampert and Merrie L. Blunk. New York: Cambridge University Press, 1998.

Saenz-Ludlow, Adalira, and Catherine Walgamuth. "Question- and Diagram-Mediated Mathematical Activity: A Case in a Fourth-Grade Classroom." *Focus on Learning Problems in Mathematics* 23, no. 4 (2001): 27–40.

Schleppegrell, Mary J. *The Language of Schooling: A Functional Linguistics Approach.* Mahwah, N.J.: Lawrence Erlbaum Associates, 2004.

Van Zoest, Laura R., ed. *Teachers Engaged in Research: Inquiry into Mathematics Classrooms, Grades 9–12.* Greenwich, Conn.: Information Age Publishing, 2006. Available from the National Council of Teachers of Mathematics.

Adding Integers: From the Classroom to the Field

Crystal A. Hill

As the last bell rings, students scurry to their respective classrooms, doors begin to close, and the class period begins. Imagine that you are in the hallway of this school and you look into an advanced mathematics class and into an Algebra 1, Part 1 mathematics class (a course designed for students who have not often found success in mathematics). What would you see? What type of instructional strategies and learning activities would you expect to take place in each of these classrooms? Research suggests that the activities in most lower-level mathematics classes require simple memory and comprehension skills, whereas classroom activities in so-called advanced classes are more likely to foster critical thinking, problem solving, and the ability to generalize (Oakes 1985). This article presents ideas for bringing higher-level thinking and learning to classes traditionally thought of as basic or remedial.

Context

This article will bring you into one of my Algebra 1, Part 1 classes to gain a more detailed description of the learners who found themselves in such a course and to demonstrate the power of using NCTM Standards–based instructional practices with such a group. The students in my class faced a diverse set of challenges. One member of the class was a student with autism, for whom it was extremely difficult to cope with not understanding the material. Several students were English language learners who struggled with the language barrier. Over half the students had an individualized education plan (IEP) for cognitive, behavioral, or emotional challenges. The high proportion of students with IEPs allowed for the assignment of a certified Exceptional Education teacher, who worked in collaboration with me to teach the course. Finally, another group of students just did not possess many of the fundamental skills of mathematics. With such an array of experiences and characteristics, the students and I faced a combination of challenges that are becoming more common in today's schools. However, despite such challenges, reflective of the NCTM's Equity Principle, I was determined to find ways to promote and maintain high expectations and provide strong support for all my students (NCTM 2000).

A Response to the Challenges

Getting back to the lesson you would have observed in my classroom as you peeked in from the hallway, the focus is on adding integers. The lesson began with me asking students to solve such problems as $7 + -1$ and $6 + 2$. I quickly realized that many students were counting on their fingers or raising their hand to ask for a calculator. One student in particular saw the addition symbol and had no concept of what it meant. Although I could have written a book on the various reasons that some of these students had made it to this course lacking very basic mathematics skills, at that moment my concern was not their divergent backgrounds and mathematical experiences but, rather, how I would teach this group of students the concept of adding integers. Do I model and conduct drill-and-practice exercises only? Do I just give a calculator to those students in need of one? How am I going to motivate students to learn basic skills that they themselves realize they should already know?

The remainder of this article describes the ways in which I responded to those challenges, providing a snapshot of activities—appropriate for a prealgebra course or a slow-paced, two-year algebra course—that foster students' understanding of integer addition. These activities were intended to meet the needs of students with diverse learning styles, for example, auditory, visual, and tactile/kinesthetic learners (Winebrenner 1996), by incorporating the use of manipulatives, visual aids, verbal cues, and an environment characterized by a lot of movement. Students who spoke little to no English were placed in groups with a student who was able to translate when needed. In the lessons leading up to these activities on integer addition, students graphed integers on the number line, found the absolute value of integers, and compared and ordered integers. The purpose of the three activities described next was to enhance the mathematics learning of this diverse group of students through motivating them and engaging them in the learning process. In addition to mathematical understanding, I wanted my students to realize that they could learn from and assist one another in learning despite the obstacles and challenges they encountered, including prior lack of success in mathematics classes; language barriers; and attention, mental, emotional, and behavioral challenges.

In addition to mathematical understanding, I wanted my students to realize that they could learn from and assist one another in learning despite the obstacles and challenges they encountered, including prior lack of success in mathematics classes; language barriers; and attention, mental, emotional, and behavioral challenges.

Activity 1: Addition with Integer Tiles

Students in groups of two were given two sets of twenty yellow and twenty red unit-square integer tiles.[1] The students were then asked to use a clean sheet of paper as an integer mat. We discussed using the tiles to model the addition of integers, with the twenty yellow tiles representing positive integers and the twenty red tiles representing negative integers.

Figure 4.1 shows the sample model of $4 + 3$ and $-4 + -3$, which was placed on the overhead projector. We discussed that the numerical expressions $4 + 3$ and $-4 + -3$ mean, respectively, to combine four items with

1. Tile spacers, which are found at many home improvement stores, are inexpensive and can be used to represent positive and negative. Integer tiles could also be made from paper.

three items and four negative items with three negative items. Next, students were asked to model the sum of each expression with their partner. Before having a teacher check their work, the students worked in pairs to model similar integer expressions and verify answers. Since their prior assessment had revealed that many students struggled with the addition of single-digit integers, within their groups students first solved expressions with same-sign addends. Having students work with numerically simple expressions strengthens their ability to manipulate same-sign addend problems before the introduction of problems with different signs.

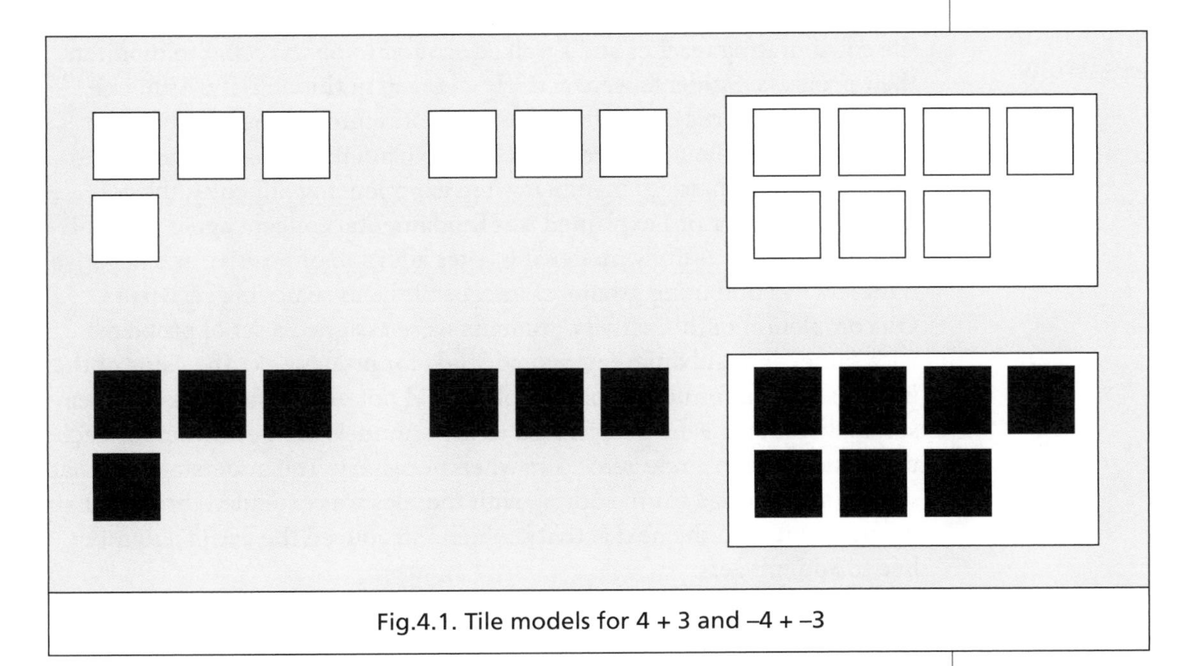

Fig.4.1. Tile models for 4 + 3 and –4 + –3

On successful completion of modeling and solving same-sign-addend expressions, I modeled the property of the *zero pair.* A zero pair is the combination of one positive (yellow) tile and one negative (red) tile. Students were asked to place three negative red tiles and two positive yellow tiles on their integer mat and to determine how many zero pairs they could create. Figure 4.2 shows the model displayed on the overhead projector.

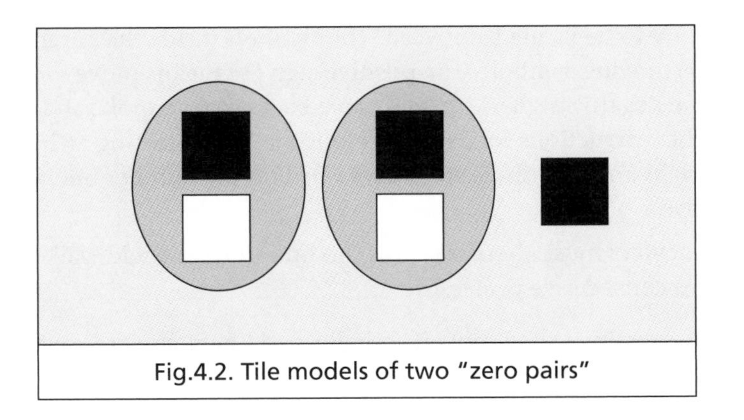

Fig.4.2. Tile models of two "zero pairs"

Starting with easier problems helped build students' confidence in their ability to add integers successfully.

Students removed the zero pairs from their integer mat and commented on what remained. This activity taught the students a fundamental concept—that removing a zero pair from the integer mat did not change the value of the tile(s) left on the mat. Students continued to work with their partners to add a set of expressions with the integer tiles. Many of these additions resulted in single-digit sums because I wanted to strengthen students' ability to work with smaller integral values before moving on to larger values. Furthermore, starting with easier problems helped build students' confidence in their ability to add integers successfully.

While students worked to model the addends and determine the sums, the collaborating teacher and I walked around to observe and to monitor their progress. Students were actively engaged in this activity. Although some students struggled with the concept of removing the zero pairs, in many instances their partner was able to explain the zero-pair concept to them. When both group members were experiencing difficulty, the collaborative teacher or I explained this fundamental concept again. Overall, the students successfully modeled integer addition of positive and negative numbers by combining groups of integer tiles and removing zero pairs. On completion of this activity, students were assigned a set of problems with same-sign and different-sign addends for homework. The value of the integers chosen for homework problems did not exceed fifteen for the reason that students were being asked to draw models of integer tiles for each expression and to circle zero pairs when necessary. The understanding that students developed from working with the tiles was extended through their involvement with the next activity, which introduced the use of a number line to add integers.

Activity 2: Walking the Line

The "Walking the Line" activity used student-created human number lines to model integer addition. In pairs, students convened outside to draw number lines on the pavement using sidewalk chalk. Each pair of students drew one number line from –10 to +10. I then gave the following instructions:

1. The first number of the expression is your starting point.
2. The operation symbol for adding (+) is the facing command, which means face forward (to the right). At the start of each problem, all students are to be facing frontward. The symbols inside the parentheses are the moving symbols. The positive sign (+) means move forward, and the negative sign (–) means move backward. (I spoke and modeled the instructions for 2 + –3, as follows: "I am starting at 2; I then turn right and take three steps backward on the number line, ending at negative 1.")
3. The partners must alternate turns; no one student could walk the line for two consecutive problems.

The expressions were spoken verbally, and I held up cards with each part of the expression written out.

As I called out the expressions and displayed them mathematically, the collaborating teacher observed each pair to determine whether they ended on the correct value. The students evaluated a set of expressions as a class. Next, each pair of students completed problems on their own, with the class determining whether they had ended on the correct value. If a pair had not ended on the correct value, any member of the class could explain the error that had been made. The activity concluded with students' completing a set of integer addition expressions on paper using a number line. The students were also given a set of addition expressions modeled erroneously on a number line and were asked to explain, in terms of the facing and moving commands, why the given answers were incorrect.

Activity 3: Taking It to the Field

This final activity was designed to connect integer addition with an everyday context. Before the introduction of this activity, students had exposure to addition problems with integers greater than 20. Both the indoor and outdoor components of this activity served as culminating experiences because they involved a variety of integer addition problems in a real-life context.

Indoor

A football field drawn on poster board and laminated with personalized team names written in each end zone was put up on the front chalkboard with magnets color-coded to denote the opposing teams. I explained that moving forward, or gaining yardage, is associated with positive integers and moving back, or losing yardage, is associated with negative integers. Each team started at the 50-yard line. Play cards were created beforehand by writing addition problems on the front of an index card and football plays resulting in a gain or loss of yardage on the back.[2] Figure 4.3 shows the front and back of a sample play card. A coin was tossed to determine the starting team. To begin, I drew a play card and showed the class the addition problem on front. If the team whose turn it was gave a correct

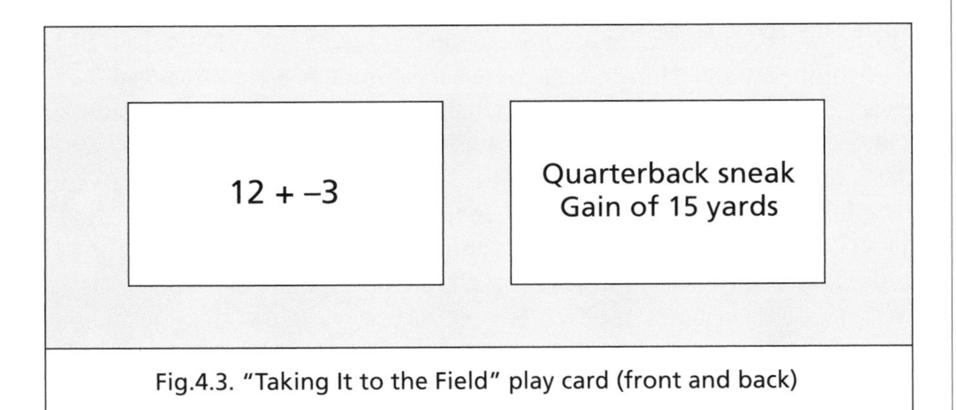

Fig.4.3. "Taking It to the Field" play card (front and back)

2. This same activity with different play cards was used throughout the school year with subtracting integers, real-number properties, and solving equations, just to name a few.

answer, they were entitled to execute the football play on the back of the card. After the play, the team had to calculate their correct field position to advance to that position. Since the students were required to calculate the field position after each play, they were continuously practicing adding integers. An incorrect response at any point led to a fumble, which meant that the ball went to the opposing team. If a team did not fumble, they were allowed two consecutive possessions.

Outdoor

The day after completing the in-class football activity, students were taken to the school's football field and everyone lined up on the 50-yard line. The collaborating teacher and I called out a combination of yardage gains and losses, and students had to walk or lightly jog to the resulting field position. For example, a gain of 10 ten yards and a loss of 15 yards would result in a field position on the 55-yard line. After a few whole-class movements, students were put into smaller groups to perform operations on the field, taking turns to model the problem and to observe the modeling. Those students who were observing determined whether their peers ended at the correct field position, and if not, a student explained where the error occurred. After completing these field exercises, students were given a set of similar problems to complete individually on paper, using the football field to model the problems if needed. The following are examples from this practice worksheet.

1. Carolina High football team has possession on the 40-yard line of the opposing team. A triple-option play is run resulting in a gain of 25 yards. What is the final field position of the ball?
2. Carolina High ran a play from the 50-yard line; they gained 30 yards, and then lost 20 yards. What is the final field position of the ball?
3. Tiger High snaps the ball at the 50-yard line, and the quarterback is sacked, resulting in a loss of 15 yards. What is the final field position of the ball?

Benefits for Students

Many of the students in this class were accustomed to a traditional approach to teaching mathematics, in which they were rarely given opportunities to be involved—cognitively or physically—in the learning process. The activities described here allowed students to become actively engaged in building and reinforcing the fundamental skill of integer addition. The students benefited from small-group and whole-class participation. The students were extremely focused in both the outdoor and classroom settings. Those for whom the activities were review worked with others who were just building their foundation of integer understanding. This team spirit became stronger the more we worked together with these activities. As a result, advanced students became more engaged and gained experience being leaders or peer teachers. An important change was that students who were just learning these concepts did not feel like they were "slow" or were somehow a burden on the class.

Using integer tiles gave students opportunities to create concrete, visual, and symbolic models of integer addition. Manipulating the tiles visually showed what happens when two same-sign or different-sign integers are added. By working together, students were able to verbalize and discuss the process of adding same-sign and different-sign integers, which helped students understand the process of integer addition. This method proved to be more successful than the use of drill-and-practice exercises without manipulatives, which had been the method used in previous years with this unit. The results in my classroom corroborate prior research (Sowell 1989) showing that students who learn operations using manipulatives outperform students who do not, as long as the teacher is knowledgeable about the manipulatives and their connection with the symbolic mathematical representation. The integer-tile activity acted as a good base from which students could transition into the "Walk the Line" and "Taking It to the Field" activities.

By working together, students were able to verbalize and discuss the process of adding same-sign and different-sign integers, which helped students understand the process of integer addition.

"Walking the Line" and "Taking It to the Field" served as bridges between students' thinking concretely and thinking abstractly about integer addition. The entire class was actively engaged because the students enjoyed working in an environment outside the classroom and making sense of the mathematics in a gamelike context. *Principles and Standards for School Mathematics* (NCTM 2000) emphasizes the importance of students' active participation as a means to develop mathematical understanding. In my experience, students with attention challenges more easily stayed engaged in activities like those described in this article because they were physically doing the mathematics and watching closely to make sure their group "performed" the expressions correctly. This activity was also very successful for beginning-level English language learners because they could model their solutions visually rather than give verbal explanations.

In my experience, students with attention challenges more easily stayed engaged in activities like those described in this article because they were physically doing the mathematics and watching closely to make sure their group "performed" the expressions correctly.

Days after the "Walking the Line" activity, while students were doing classwork, I heard them referring back to the commands used for this activity; they were cognitively visualizing themselves on the number line without actually being outside. "Taking It to the Field" provided a real-life context for integer addition, which was a great source of motivation for students. Students in the class who played football or had knowledge of the sport were able to give an overview of the game to those who lacked that understanding. Through these real-life explanations, some students realized that they had a better understanding of integer addition than they initially thought.

Conclusion

As you can see from this glimpse into my classroom, these activities represented a nontraditional approach to learning integer addition. The outcome was that students were fully engaged and even became enthusiastic about learning the fundamental skill of integer addition. To see this diverse group of students share in the excitement of, and demonstrate enthusiasm for, learning mathematical skills and concepts was rewarding for me. As they got into the activities and began to make sense of the mathematics, the students were no longer concerned that they had encountered this knowledge in previous courses. Remarkably, the more engaged they became in these activities, the less reliant they were on the calculators they had all clamored for at the start. I believe that this outcome resulted from an increase in their mathematical understanding and a corresponding increase in their confidence in their ability to add integers. As they progressed through the year in my class, this confidence was leveraged as we moved into more advanced topics, such as integer subtraction and solving two-step equations. I found the students more ready and willing to learn as the school year progressed.

Epilogue

As the period ends and you now leave the Algebra 1, Part 1 classroom, imagine how different the students' experiences would have been if only "traditional" pedagogical methods had been used. How many of them would have been left out? Which ones would have spent another year in mathematics without acquiring the basic skill of integer addition or the concept of zero pairs? As you turn to walk away from the classroom door, you smile, knowing that the needs of this diverse and often underserved group of students were met. One brick of a strong mathematical foundation was laid into place for each of them.

REFERENCES

National Council of Teachers of Mathematics (NCTM). *Principles and Standards for School Mathematics.* Reston, Va.: NCTM, 2000.

Oakes, Jeannie. *Keeping Track: How Schools Structure Inequality*. New York: Vail-Ballou Press, 1985.

Sowell, Evelyn J. "Effects of Manipulative Materials in Mathematics Instruction." *Journal for Research in Mathematics Education* 20 (November 1989): 498–505.

Winebrenner, Susan. *Teaching Kids with Learning Difficulties in the Regular Classroom: Strategies and Techniques Every Teacher Can Use to Challenge and Motivate Struggling Students.* Minneapolis, Minn.: Free Spirit Publishing, 1996.

5

The Human Graph Project: Giving Students Mathematical Power through Differentiated Instruction

David K. Pugalee
Adam Harbaugh
Lan Hue Quach

DIFFERENTIATION in mathematics teaching can help the classroom teacher reach several important instructional goals—including the use of research-based approaches that have been shown to help students with learning challenges master mathematics content in the general education environment (Fuchs and Fuchs 2001). Such practices incorporate multiple instructional activities characterized by high levels of engagement, challenging achievement standards, self-verbalization processes, and physical and verbal representations of concepts or problem-solving processes. This article presents a differentiated lesson whose activities address multiple student learning characteristics. In particular, because the classroom in which the lesson was implemented contained a large number of English language learners (ELLs), the discussion includes information about meeting the needs of these students.

According to George (2005), the best teachers "have always recognized that every student is unique and, to a degree, deserves and requires special attention and adaptation of the learning experience to fit those unique needs" (p. 189). Given the increasing diversity in schools today, differentiation of instruction in the mathematics classroom has become not only important but necessary. Teachers working in heterogeneous classrooms are not only required to meet the academic needs of students at different levels of academic achievement and from different socioeconomic backgrounds; they must also address the needs of nonnative English speakers, otherwise known as ELLs (Atunez 2002; Nieto 2002; Thomas and Collier 2002). Although the number of ELLs has grown exponentially on both national and state levels (Ruiz-de-Velasco and Fix 2000), these students continue to demonstrate lower academic achievement than their native-English-speaking peers (Moss and Puma 1995). In addition, researchers have argued that the instructional strategies used by most mainstream classroom teachers do not adequately support the needs of many students (Nieto 2002), especially those of ELLs (Menken and Atunez 2001; Walqui 1999). To meet the needs of diverse learners effectively, educators must acknowledge the differences in their classrooms by considering students' interests, strengths, and weaknesses at all stages of instructional planning and in the use of assessments (Lawrence-Brown 2004).

Defining Differentiated Instruction: A Focus on Process

The use of differentiated instruction—described by Tomlinson (2004, p. 8) as "ensuring that what a student learns, how he/she learns it, and how the student demonstrates what he/she has learned is a match for that student's readiness, interests, and preferred mode of learning"—becomes crucial in teaching for mathematical understanding. One way in which to differentiate instruction is to focus on the learning *process* (Tomlinson 2001). Differentiation in process involves modifying the instructional activities so as to move individual students successfully from their current understanding to a more complex level of understanding.

Tomlinson and McTighe (2006) identified three pathways along which teachers can think about differentiating the learning process:

1. select strategies that build on students' readiness, interests, and learning preferences;
2. guide students in understanding how to use the approaches effectively; and
3. help students reflect on what strategies work best for them as learners.

When differentiating process by considering students' readiness, teachers carefully connect each student's current level of understanding with the difficulty of the task. Differentiating process by considering students' interests allows students both a voice and a choice in the tasks in which they will engage. By considering the diverse ways in which students learn best, teachers can also choose to differentiate process by allowing students to construct meaning using their preferred way of learning. In the following example, we describe the way in which one eighth-grade mathematics teacher differentiated process on the basis of the readiness and learning preferences of his students.

By considering the diverse ways in which students learn best, teachers can also choose to differentiate process by allowing students to construct meaning using their preferred way of learning.

A Sense-Making Activity: The Human Graph Project

Background

In its Representation Standard, the National Council of Teachers of Mathematics (NCTM 2000) suggests that teachers provide students with opportunities to develop an understanding of multiple representations for algebraic phenomena, including equations, graphs, and tables. Students need to develop fluency with constructing and interpreting these various representations. Friel and her colleagues (2001) offer a series of exemplar activities in which students are asked to consider both graphic and verbal representations. In these complementary activities, students are first asked to tell a story by interpreting a graph and then asked to construct a graph based on a given story.

Cartesian coordinate graphs are one of many important and connected external, and sometimes internal, representations (Goldin and Kaput 1996) that help constitute many concepts in algebra and geometry. Goldin and Kaput describe how the mathematical idea symbolically represented by the equation $y = -3x + 6$ has multiple representations, each of which is a connected and constituent part of the mathematical concept of linear relationship. The equation may represent the table of x and y values as shown in figure 5.1. This equation may also correspond to the following written representations:

> the relation between position and time of an object moving west with a constant velocity of 3 meters per second, beginning 6 meters east of the origin, or it might represent the hypotenuse of a right triangle ... whose base is 2 units long and whose height is 6 units. (Goldin and Kaput 1996, p. 400)

The equation may also correspond to a line with slope of –3 and intersecting the y-axis at the point (0, 6), as shown in figure 5.1.

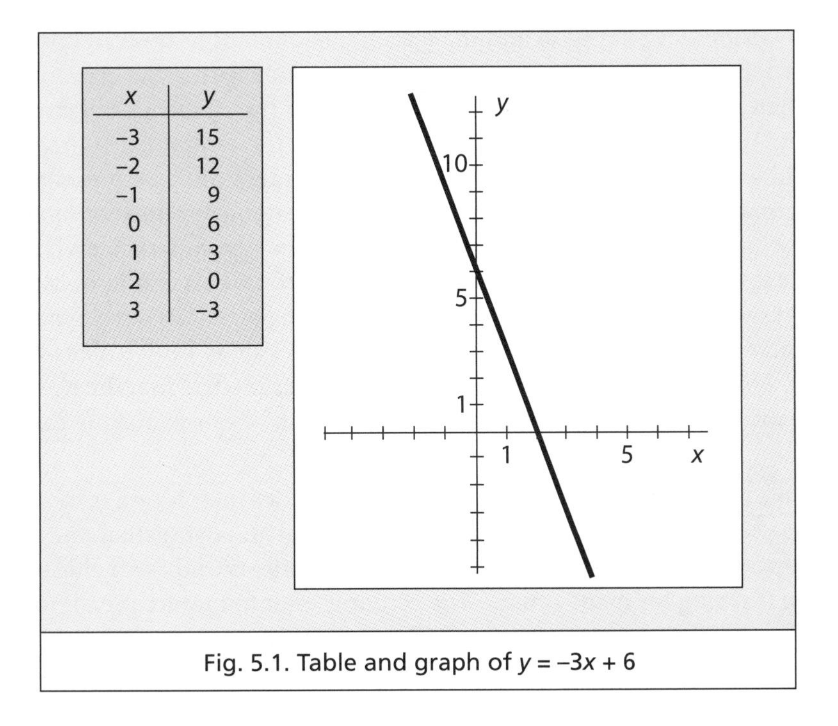

x	y
–3	15
–2	12
–1	9
0	6
1	3
2	0
3	–3

Fig. 5.1. Table and graph of $y = -3x + 6$

Graphical representation is one of several pieces to the mathematical puzzle. The concept of graphing equations and functions on the Cartesian plane is an important one for students in the middle grades to understand. This concept is essential for a deep understanding of many ideas in algebra, which the majority of middle school students are exposed to before they enter high school. A solid understanding of graphing algebraic equations and functions can support further understanding of advanced mathematical topics, such as concepts and ideas in trigonometry and calculus.

Graphing and related concepts are traditionally introduced to students beginning with definitions and nomenclature of the basic structure and components of the Cartesian coordinate system. Teachers may then choose to show examples of points or ordered pairs plotted on the coordinate axes followed by some individual practice by the students until they have mastered plotting points in each of the four quadrants. From this foundation, teachers move on to having students learn to graph linear equations through different methods, likely including some discussion of slope and the y-intercept (e.g., how to find them and what they mean for the graph of a line). In many classrooms, these and other related activities are likely accomplished using paper-and-pencil assignments that follow a standard learning sequence: teacher-led demonstration, examples, guided practice, and individual practice.

Although each of the activities above is important to developing an initial understanding of graphing linear and nonlinear relationships, the way in which they are organized and presented leaves many middle school students without the necessary understanding of important introductory ideas (Zehler 1994; Kaufman 2004). For the ELL, as well as many other students, methods that are teacher-centered and that employ decontextualized tasks that place a heavy emphasis on individual learning can hinder the development of English and the learning of content in several ways. These approaches often fail to promote interactions within the classroom with native English speakers and leave ELLs with the challenge of learning content without adequate visual support needed for comprehension. For the ELLs to learn English for comprehension, content must be presented in a meaningful context and activities must include opportunities for interactions with native English speakers. Much research has shown that when ELLs are encouraged to work in supportive environments and in meaningful ways with their mainstream peers, second-language (L2) development is greatly enhanced (Cummins 2001; Nieto 2000; Valdes 1996; Valenzuela 1999). Through the differentiation of mathematics instruction, the needs of ELLs and other diverse students are considered in advance, making the lesson more likely to engage all students fully.

One approach to differentiation in mathematics instruction is to include activities that enrich students' conceptual and contextual understanding—serving as reinforcement for some students and as an alternative way of learning for many others.

One approach to differentiation in mathematics instruction is to include activities that enrich students' conceptual and contextual understanding—serving as reinforcement for some students and as an alternative way of learning for many others. The activities that follow are meant to provide alternative approaches to traditional methods for teaching graphing concepts at and beyond the introductory algebra level. Teachers should decide, on the basis of the needs of their students, to what degree the activities should accompany or replace more traditional approaches. These activities, with various modifications, have been used by the authors in middle and secondary school classrooms with great success, especially for students learning English as a second language.

The Human Graph

The Human Graph activity (Bay and Wasman 2000) is a natural transformation of small-scale, pencil-and-paper mathematics to a larger scale in which the Cartesian coordinate system is represented on the floor of a gymnasium, cafeteria, or classroom using tape or outdoors in a parking lot or field using spray paint or chalk. This activity is powerful for ELLs in particular because it allows students to engage actively and physically in the construction of the graph and representations of linear and nonlinear algebraic relationships. Teachers should model the same standards they expect when creating the coordinate axes; the axes should be constructed with straight and perpendicular line segments. Allowing ELLs to participate in the construction of the line segments gives them the opportunity to be successful at a task and helps create a sense of belonging in an academic setting. Teachers may choose not to label the scale explicitly so that they can change the scaling for various graphing situations. When the labeling is necessary, teachers can allow beginning-level ELLs to complete this task. Again, these small acts of inclusion of ELLs in the mainstream classroom can facilitate future L2 development. Research on the affective dimensions of L2 development shows that learning is best facilitated in classrooms in which the affective filter[1] is low (Krashen, 1994, 1982). In other words, student anxiety hinders the development of a second language. When students feel included and a part of a classroom, they are more likely to engage in activities that support comprehension.

Figure 5.2 shows a small group of students graphing the equation $y = -2x - 3$ on a field where the coordinate axes were spray-painted on the ground using string as a guide (and *after* applying the Pythagorean

Fig. 5.2. Third-story view of students graphing $y = -2x - 3$

1. *Affect* is defined as "the effect of personality motivation and other 'affective variables' on second language acquisition" (Krashen 1994, p. 57). The Affective Filter hypothesis, according to Krashen (1982), asserts that a number of affective variables, such as motivation, self-confidence, and anxiety, play a facilitative but noncausal role in second-language acquisition. In other words, second-language development is facilitated when the learner has a low level of anxiety.

theorem to ensure that the axes were constructed at right angles!). In this particular example, ELLs were asked to help the teacher measure and create the points on both the x- and y-axes. One newcomer was invited to join the teacher on the school's third floor, from which some of the photos of the result were taken, an experience that helped make this student feel supported and involved with the class activity.

If the human graph activity is used to introduce graphing concepts to students, teachers will have to decide how much emphasis is placed on naming and defining such terms as *ordered pair, Cartesian coordinate system, x-axis, y-axis, point,* and *line*. Students need to be equipped with a common, mathematically accurate vocabulary to effectively communicate with one another and the teacher. Because vocabulary development is essential to the acquisition of academic language, teachers must be explicit in their use of important terms with ELLs. In the scenario presented here, with his ELLs in mind, the teacher introduced the terms above, with visuals when appropriate, before presenting the outside graphing task. Students were then allowed to create and illustrate a set of cards (large index cards or cut cardstock) that they could take home to review. Depending on the level of proficiency of the ELLs in the class, teachers could also allow students the opportunities to create and play games with important vocabulary to reinforce their understanding.

What follows are suggested directions for a class of twenty-five to thirty students. Many teachers will want to amend these directions to suit the needs of their individual classroom situation and to accommodate the students in their classroom. Some specific suggestions accompany the activity description.

Implementing the activity

This activity begins with an exercise in plotting points so that, when taken together, the students form a prescribed line. Exercises in transformations of $y = x$ then follow. In preparation for the graphing activity, the teacher should evenly divide the class into groups of ten to thirteen students; more than this number per group may cause difficulties in group interactions, as well as in placing all students in the graph. Teachers with larger class sizes could modify this activity by dividing the class into large groups and using more than one set of coordinate axes.

As described previously, these sets of axes could also be created by the students, adding another element of ownership and inquiry to the activity. How long do the axes need to be? What is the best scale for the axes? How can we be sure that the axes are perpendicular? Each of these questions is necessary for students to consider in creating the axes. This student involvement can help illuminate important aspects of graphing that translate well to the classroom—the types of insights that may be taken for granted if the teacher simply provides a set of axes on paper, the ground, or the floor.

Another possible modification, if space for multiple sets of axes is not practical, is that teachers can have one set of students represent the graph while the others act as recorders and are asked to make a sketch of the graph, write the equation represented, draw a table consisting of the ordered pairs occupied by their classmates, and write a description of the graph. Incorporating each of these forms of representation would create opportunities for students to make meaningful connections between the concrete and abstract ideas associated with algebraic representations and to gain a better understanding of the algebraic phenomenon described by each.

After dividing the class into groups, the teacher then distributes index cards with numbers written on the back; these numbers are the x-values for the ordered pairs each student will plot to form the line. On the other side of the index card is written the equation of a line. Students will have to use their x-value and the equation to determine their corresponding y-value. To support the ELLs further, the cards might also include a small visual to remind them which is the x-axis and which the y-axis (see fig. 5.3 as an example). We suggest that these preparatory activities be done in the classroom on the day of the activity or the day before. The length of these activities will vary depending on students, the depth of discussion, and the duration of the class period.

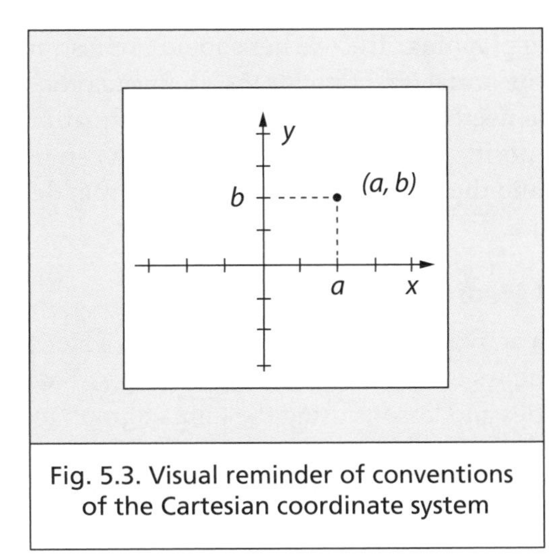

Fig. 5.3. Visual reminder of conventions of the Cartesian coordinate system

Once everyone in the group has determined their ordered pair, the group with cards can plot themselves to form the line. While they are standing in place, they then should be instructed to face in a direction perpendicular to the line that they have created and extend their arms out in the direction on the line. By doing so, the group actually connects the ordered pairs, forming a continuous line rather than a discrete set of points. ELLs with limited English proficiency can be paired with more advanced ELLs or native English speakers with strong linguistic skills when completing aspects of this or other tasks that may be more challenging.

Teachers may want to discuss with the class the difference between the graphs before and after the students aligned themselves and extended their arms. This discussion would offer an opportunity to make connections between discrete and continuous graphs. The class may have prior knowledge about plotting functions of natural numbers or real numbers. This discussion may benefit students who may not have understood why one cannot connect the points of the graph if the domain is the number of students, or why one can do so if the domain is time. The strength of having this discussion while students are physically standing on the graph, or while they observe their classmates doing so, is that it offers the natural reinforcement of visual in addition to verbal representation of ideas. This visual support helps not only the ELLs in the class but also students with different levels of prior knowledge or those for whom pencil-and-paper representations are still too abstract to carry much meaning.

After students have made the first graph, the next exercise has students plotting assigned ordered pairs—without being given an equation—that, when taken together, create a line. Students are given another index card with an ordered pair, and the group is instructed to plot themselves on the coordinate system. Once plotted, the students are asked to determine the equation of their line while maintaining their positions. Teachers may have discussed slope and y-intercepts with the class before this exercise, although having students plot points and form curves on the human graph can be an effective, informal environment to initiate discussions of concepts surrounding graphing. The teacher should orchestrate the discussion by giving some initial direction for their conversation, such as asking, “What do you need to know to determine the equation?” or “Who is standing at a key position on the graph?” Discussion can focus on helping students understand the role of slope and y-intercept in determining the equation of the line.

Extensions and Modifications of the Activity

The human graph activity should be considered as an alternative to more traditional approaches of teaching graphing concepts. Teachers should tailor their activities and lessons using the human graph to fit their instructional goals or learning targets. The human graph can also be used effectively at the secondary school level to introduce polynomial, exponential, and trigonometric functions, among others.

When introducing the concept of transformations of the parent function (in this instance, the equation $y = x$), teachers can return to the human graph as a shared learning experience that may have been used previously with the class for more elementary aspects of graphing. Applying their prior knowledge of graphing, students can extend their understanding of the relationships among symbolic, numerical, and graphical representations of classes of linear equations (e.g., $y = x$, $y = 2x$, and $y = 2x - 3$).

Another alternative setting for learning graphing concepts is with Internet-based virtual environments. For instance, the National Library of Virtual Manipulatives (nlvm.usu.edu/en/nav/vlibrary.html) offers several applets that students can use to experiment with several conjectures about graphing, and the Shodor Center (www.shodor.org/interactivate/activities/SlopeSlider) offers an interactive applet to explore changes in slope. As with the human graph activity, teachers can use this alternative environment to supplement or replace traditional pencil-and-paper-based activities. To accommodate all learners, teachers may want to use more than one of these approaches. Considering time concerns that using three or more ways to teach graphing ideas would create, teachers should be conscious of the multiple concepts and objectives that can be embedded within the activities. Teachers should clearly identify appropriate multiple learning targets that can be addressed through such differentiated activities.

A Teacher's Voice

A middle-grades teacher who has used the Human Graphing activity commented,

> I have found this activity very helpful to students who have not mastered graphing points or who do not understand linear functions. Instead of looking at a sheet of graph paper and trying to understand graphing, students are physically part of the graph. They must figure out how to position themselves to meet the conditions of the function. If one of the students is out of line, the students, together, learn how to move the person to the correct location. While they are making the graph, I call on students to tell me the names of students who are located on a particular point or the students located on the points representing the outputs for various inputs. Students also do more traditional exercises to reinforce the concepts from the activity, but this hands-on component builds strong conceptual understanding. This different approach is especially effective with my students who are still learning English (Personal conversation, March 24, 2006).

Conclusion

Differentiating instruction hits at the heart of NCTM's (2000) Equity Principle, which states that excellence in mathematics requires "high expectations and strong support for all students" (p. 12). With the increasing numbers of ELLs in schools, having high expectations of learners who struggle to speak, understand, read, and write in the language of instruction, and supporting language development while teaching content, can be great challenges. The differentiation of process recognizes that all students must have opportunities to learn mathematics in an environment that is supportive yet challenging. Such differentiation of instruction is important for the ELL because it acknowledges the diversity that each student brings to the classroom rather than frames these learners as deficient. In addition, these practices—

- support second-language development by allowing ELLs to interact meaningfully with native speakers of English in both structured and unstructured contexts,
- recognize and include ELLs as contributing members of the classroom, and
- create opportunities to apply their newly acquired knowledge in exciting and contextualized ways.

Ultimately, the Human Graph Project is an example of a differentiation of process that allows teachers to create alternative opportunities to learn through active engagement in the construction of the graph and of representations of linear and nonlinear algebraic relationships. Most important, through the use of appropriate modifications for diverse learners (i.e. the use of visuals, kinesthetic learning strategies, opportunities for pair or group work, and so on), this activity allows teachers to move students from their current understanding of graphing to a more complex level. Students who struggle are given multiple opportunities to reinforce important mathematical concepts with practice and application. Students who have higher readiness levels can support struggling learners throughout the group activity and be challenged by additional extension activities.

The shared goal of this activity is to provide students the opportunity to apply their prior knowledge of graphing and extend their understanding of the relationships among symbolic, numerical, and graphical representations of classes of linear equations while acknowledging the differences in students' prior experiences and knowledge. Activities that differentiate process in the mathematics classroom should emphasize important mathematical concepts; provide explicit means to assess students' understanding; be flexible in the use of pairs, small groups, large groups, and individual work; and infuse engaging tasks that offer opportunities for students to be participatory learners. Such practices create essential opportunities for students to develop mathematical power through sense-making activities.

REFERENCES

Antunez, Beth. "The Preparation and Professional Development of Teachers of English Language Learners." *ERIC Digest*. Washington, D.C.: ERIC Clearinghouse on Teaching and Teacher Education, 2002. ERIC Document #ED477724. Available online at www.ericdigests.org/2004-1/english.htm.

Bay, Jennifer M., and Deanna G. Wasman. "Sharing Teaching Ideas: Making the Coordinate Grid Come to Life with Human Graphing." *Mathematics Teacher* 93 (2000): 553–54.

Cummins, Jim. *Language, Power, and Pedagogy*. Cleveland: Multilingual Matters, 2001.

Friel, Susan, Sid Rachlin, Dorothy Doyle, Claire Nygard, David Pugalee, and Mark Ellis. *Navigating through Algebra in Grades 6–8. Principles and Standards for School Mathematics* Navigations Series. Reston, Va.: National Council of Teachers of Mathematics, 2001.

Fuchs, Lynn S., and Douglas Fuchs. "Principles for the Prevention and Intervention of Mathematics Difficulties." *Learning Disabilities Research and Practice* 16, no. 2 (2001): 85–95.

George, Paul S. "A Rationale for Differentiating Instruction in the Regular Classroom." *Theory into Practice* 44, no. 3 (2005): 185–93.

Goldin, Gerald A., and James J. Kaput. "A Joint Perspective on the Idea of Representation in Learning and Doing Mathematics." In *Theories of Mathematical Learning,* edited by Leslie P. Steffe and Pearla Nesher, pp. 397–430. Mahwah, N.J.: Lawrence Erlbaum Associates, 1996.

Kaufman, Dorit. "Constructivist Issues in Language Learning and Teaching." *Annual Review of Applied Linguistics* 24 (2004): 303–19.

Krashen, Stephen D. *Principles and Practice in Second-Language Learning and Acquisition.* Oxford: Pergamon, 1982.

———. "Bilingual Education and Second-Language Acquisition Theory." In Bilingual Education Office (ed.), *Schooling and Language-Minority Students: A Theoretical Framework,* 2nd ed., edited by the California State Department of Education, pp. 47–75. Los Angeles: Evaluation Dissemination and Assessment Center, California State University, 1994.

Lawrence-Brown, Diana. "Differentiated Instruction: Inclusive Strategies for Standards-Based Learning That Benefit the Whole Class." *American Secondary Education* 32 (2004): 34–62.

Menken, Kate, and Beth Atunez. *An Overview of the Preparation and Certification of Teachers Working with Limited English Proficient (LEP) Students.* Washington, D.C.: National Clearinghouse for Bilingual Education and ERIC Clearinghouse on Teaching and Teacher Education. Retrieved May 15, 2003, from www.ericsp.org/pages/digests/ncbe.pdf.

Moss, Marc, and Michael Puma. *Prospects: The Congressionally Mandated Study of Educational Growth and Opportunity.* First-year report on language minority and limited English proficient students. Washington, D.C.: U.S. Department of Education, 1995.

National Council of Teachers of Mathematics (NCTM). *Principles and Standards for School Mathematics.* Reston, Va.: NCTM, 2000.

Nieto, Sonia. *Affirming Diversity: The Sociopolitical Context of Multicultural Education.* New York: Longman, 2002.

———. *Language, Culture, and Teaching: Critical Perspectives for a New Century: A Compilation of Previously Published Journal Articles and Book Chapters.* Mahwah, N.J.: Lawrence Erlbaum Associates, 2002.

Ruiz-de-Velasco, Jorge, and Michael Fix *Overlooked and Underserved: Immigrant Students in U.S. Secondary Schools.* Washington, D.C.: Urban Institute, 2000.

Thomas, Wayne P., and Virginia P. Collier. "A National Study of School Effectiveness for Language Minority Students' Long-Term Academic Achievement." Berkeley, Calif.: Center for Research of Education, Diversity, and Excellence, 2002. Retrieved February 9, 2005, from www.crede.org/research/llaa/ 1.1 final.html.

Tomlinson, Carol A. *How to Differentiate Instruction in Mixed-Ability Classrooms.* 2nd ed. Alexandria, Va.: Association for Supervision and Curriculum Development, 2001.

———. "Sharing Responsibility for Differentiating Instruction." *Roeper Review* 26, no. 4 (2004): 188–89.

Tomlinson, Carol A., and Jay McTighe. *Integrating Differentiated Instruction and Understanding by Design.* Alexandria, Va.: Association for Supervision and Curriculum Development, 2006.

Valdés, Gudalupe. *Con Respeto: Bridging the Distances between Culturally Diverse Families and Schools: An Ethnographic Portrait.* New York: Teachers College Press, 1996.

Valenzuela, Angela. *Subtractive Schooling: U.S.–Mexican Youth and the Politics of Caring.* Albany: State University of New York Press, 1999.

Walqui, Aida. "Professional Development for Teachers of English Language Learners." Paper presented at an invitational conference sponsored by the National Educational Research Policy and Priorities Board, the Office of Educational Research and Improvement, and the Office of Bilingual Education and Minority Languages Affairs, Washington, D.C., July 1999.

Zehler, Annette. *Working with English Language Learners: Strategies for Elementary and Middle School Teachers.* National Clearinghouse for English Language Acquisition (NCELA) Program Information Guide Series, Number 19. Washington, D.C.: NCELA, 1994 .

6

What Does That Mean? Drawing on Latino and Latina Students' Language and Culture to Make Mathematical Meaning

Sylvia Celedón-Pattichis

PRINCIPLES and Standards for School Mathematics (NCTM 2000) suggests that teachers set high expectations and render strong support for *all* students to have opportunities to learn mathematics. The issue of opportunities to learn is particularly pertinent for English language learners (ELLs) because they are more likely to be "victims of low expectations" (NCTM 2000, p. 13). When ELLs enroll in schools in the United States, they face many challenges. These students worry not only about fitting in culturally and linguistically but also about performing well in such content areas as mathematics. They need teachers who are strong advocates (Fu 1995).

Previous research has focused on understanding the importance of discourse between teachers and students in bilingual elementary school mathematics classrooms (Khisty 1995) and in elementary classrooms having ELLs and a monolingual English-speaking teacher (Khisty and Chval 2002). Other research has contributed to studies of bilingual learners in mathematics, showing the benefits of students' code-switching (i.e., alternating between languages) and identifying ways that teachers can support student discourse (Moschkovich 1999). However, we find a paucity of research that specifically addresses issues regarding the learning of mathematics by ELLs using standards-based curricula at the secondary school level.

This lack of information can be attributed to some perceptions in English as a second language (ESL) education that because ELLs have difficulty with the second language, they should study the areas of language arts intensively at the expense of other content areas. This view seems to be true given California's Proposition 227 and Arizona's Proposition 203, which mandate that beginning ELL students be exposed to English for one year, denying them access to the rest of the curriculum.

The author would like to thank the reviewers and editors for their thoughtful comments on this article, which was strengthened by their feedback.

The goal of this study was to analyze how Mrs. Brown[1], a middle school ESL/mathematics teacher, used students' language and culture to support their learning of English and mathematics. More specifically, I was interested in how Spanish and English were used to develop mathematical concepts (i.e., clarity or ambiguity of language) and how students' daily experiences were used as resources in the classroom. Khisty (1995) addressed the use of language through observing bilingual fifth-grade classrooms in which mathematics was taught. However, the study described herein attempted to answer this question at the secondary school level (sixth to eighth grade), where a gap exists in the literature about the role of language and culture in mathematics.

In the sections that follow I discuss first the NCTM Standards as they relate to language minority students. Second, I present the context of the classroom case. Third, I perform a detailed analysis of the findings with samples of teacher-student discourse to discuss how the students' language and culture were used in ways that supported students' mathematical meaning making. Finally, I end with a discussion of the conclusions and implications of this study for teachers of mathematics who work with English language learners.

Background

NCTM recognizes the importance of making mathematics accessible to bilingual and other culturally and linguistically diverse students. In its position statement on mathematics for language minority students, NCTM (1993) proposed the following:

- All students, regardless of their language or cultural background, must study a core curriculum in mathematics based on the NCTM Standards.
- Educators must identify and remove language-based barriers.
- Language-minority students must be given appropriate assistance in learning mathematics.
- Counselors and teachers must support and encourage students in continuing their mathematics education.
- The importance of mathematics and the nature of the mathematics program must be communicated to both students and parents.
- The mathematics curriculum must include connections to the cultural heritage of students.
- Teaching and assessment strategies must build on the cultural heritage and learning styles of students.

With this position statement, NCTM explicitly calls for attention to groups of students who are not included in the mainstream population. Because many ELLs tend to experience a mismatch between the language used at home and the language used at school (Heath, 1983; Wells, 1987), these students can be made to feel more comfortable—and thereby given greater

1. All names are pseudonyms.

access to opportunities to learn (Tate 2005)—by including their culture and language in the mathematics classroom.

Context of the Classroom Case

This qualitative study was conducted for approximately one-and-a-half years in an urban public school, Red Middle School, located in central Texas. According to Texas Education Agency (1996) statistics, more than 1,000 students were enrolled in the school, predominantly Latino and Latina. More than 70 percent of the students were economically disadvantaged, and 5 percent were in bilingual/ESL programs. Although Red Middle School had a small percent of students in bilingual/ESL programs, Mrs. Brown's classroom was a self-contained classroom that consisted only of students learning English as a second language.

Participants

The Teacher

Mrs. Brown, the ESL/mathematics teacher, was selected for this study because she taught mathematics to ELLs. Hers was a unique case because she had used a traditional mathematics curriculum during the first year I observed her class, but during the second year she implemented units from the Connected Mathematics Project (CMP), a reform-based curriculum that was part of her district's systemic reform initiative[2]. Since the CMP materials required more inquiry and explanation from students, this shift allowed me to document the successes and struggles faced by the teacher and the students as they worked to develop different patterns of interaction (see Celedón-Pattichis [2001]).

At the time of the study, Mrs. Brown had taught for almost five years. She perceived her responsibilities as a teacher working with ELLs to be twofold—to teach English and to teach mathematics content:

The teacher perceived her responsibilities working with ELLs to be twofold—to teach English and to teach mathematics content.

> I don't discourage them [the students] speaking Spanish in either of the classes [beginners and advanced level]. I try to encourage them to speak English, but I don't discourage them from speaking Spanish. Like, I try to focus on the math and/or..... This is a change from what I was doing three years ago. I was trying to focus on the English and I was thinking, "Well, you know, once they get to a math class, then they'll get more math." But my main goal then was to get them to speak in English. But then I realized that they were so behind in math that they would never, ever be able to survive in a math class. So I realized that I needed to be focusing on the math, too. But the two most important things for me to teach them, while they are with me, are the English and the math.

This quote acknowledges that most ESL teachers in earlier decades focused primarily on developing students' English language proficiency. The

2. Visit the Show Me Center at showmecenter.missouri.edu for more information about NSF-funded middle school mathematics curricula.

content-area learning, such as mathematics, tended to be given less priority (Thomas and Collier 1997). Mrs. Brown realized that such an approach was a disservice to ELLs because they would fall behind once they were mainstreamed to mathematics classes.

The Students

Mrs. Brown's class consisted of a sample of 22 middle school students of Latino descent (from Mexico, Nicaragua, El Salvador, and Honduras) who were identified as English language learners by their teacher and by their scores on the Language Assessment Battery (Texas Education Agency 1996). The students in Mrs. Brown's class were in a self-contained ESL/ mathematics class, which meant that sixth through eighth graders were taught in the same classroom. The total number of students in the class varied throughout the semester because students who became English proficient were transitioned into regular or honors mathematics courses. The students' English proficiency ranged from beginning to advanced levels.

Data Collection

To analyze and document the types of communication patterns used by the teacher and her students in the classroom, I visited Mrs. Brown's classroom for one-and-a-half years at least twice a week to audiotape and observe the lessons. Data from these observations were used to identify and analyze specific classroom events. In particular, seven audiotaped lessons were selected and transcribed for in-depth analysis. (See table 6.1 for transcription conventions.)

Table 6.1
Transcription Conventions (Adapted from Green and Wallat [1981])

T	Teacher
S	Student responds
Ss	Students respond chorally
Plain font	English
Bold	**Spanish**
Italics	*Translation of Spanish into English* (not said by the teacher; just for reader)
XXX	TEACHER'S TALK
Xxx	Student's talk
{ }	Inaudible messages
(( ))	Nonverbal information
[ ]	Overlapped information
...	Pause or continuation of a thought
!	Indicates emphasis or higher pitch at the end of a phrase

Classroom Learning Context

The students in Mrs. Brown's classroom experienced a shift from the traditional curriculum to the reform-based curriculum in the second year of the study. As part of the new curriculum, students often worked in pairs or groups on solving contextualized problems that were typically embedded in a story or narrative. In making the transition from a traditional to a reform-based curriculum, the teacher and students often expressed how difficult it was to "think differently," which meant that students were expected to explain their reasoning orally and in writing and the teacher was expected to pose questions that would elicit responses that got at students' mathematical thinking, not just their solutions.

In a reform-based curriculum, the teacher and students often expressed how difficult it was to "think differently," which meant that students were expected to explain their reasoning orally and in writing and the teacher was expected to pose questions that would elicit responses that got at students' mathematical thinking, not just their solutions.

Typical lessons from the reform-based Connected Mathematics Project units included investigations that consisted of three phases (Lappan et al. 1996b): (1) launching, (2) exploring, and (3) summarizing. During launching, the teacher engaged students as a whole class in thinking about and generating information that was relevant to them. The teacher also helped students understand the context of the story and the mathematical problem being posed. In exploring, the teacher allowed students to work individually, in pairs, in groups, or as a class, depending on the nature of the problem. The students' roles during this phase consisted of collecting data, sharing ideas with their peers, looking for patterns, making conjectures, and developing problem-solving strategies. The teacher's role involved checking for understanding of the problem by observing students and posing scaffolding questions or comments that would encourage them to persevere on the problem or nudge them in a mathematically more productive direction. For summarizing, students were expected to synthesize the class information and to make conjectures about mathematical concepts and relationships that they had explored and begun to make sense of. Examples are shown in the following section.

Findings

Throughout my observations, Mrs. Brown proved very adept at engaging students by drawing on their cultural and linguistic backgrounds. This skill, together with a more inquiry-oriented curriculum in the second year, led to greater levels of student participation in her mathematics classroom. Specifically, three themes that emerged from the data are presented to illustrate the ways in which the teacher drew on students' culture and language to make connections with mathematics. One involves drawing on students' identities and experiences to engage them in learning mathematics. The second includes the use of cognates to help ELLs transfer mathematical meaning from Spanish to English. The third is the use of conceptually based games to allow students opportunities to communicate with mathematical language in a nonthreatening environment.

Drawing on Students' Identities and Experiences

The teacher in this study often drew on students' identities and experiences to make connections with the curriculum (Gonzalez, Moll, and Amanti

2005). For example, to launch the study of data analysis and measures of center (mean, median, mode), Mrs. Brown engaged students in a short discussion about their names. Students were asked, "Do you know anything interesting about how you were named or about the history behind the family's name?" (see Lappan et al. [1996a]). Typical answers from students included, "I was named after my father" or "My parents chose to give me a relative's name." Other students engaged in this discussion by sharing with the teacher that their parents chose names that represented a significant event. For example, Esperanza shared that her mother had had problems in the process of giving birth, so she named her with the Spanish word for *Hope*. Although this student tended to be shy in class, this discussion provided opportunities for her to engage in sharing something that was significant to her identity.

After this brief introductory discussion, Mrs. Brown asked students to get a sticky note and write on it the number of letters in their names. During this activity students were also encouraged to think about a situation in which name length would matter (e.g., having a long name might be a disadvantage when completing a form because it might have a limit on the number of letters). The class then discussed how they were going to define the length of the name, and everyone decided to include the first and last name. After this discussion, students collected data about their names and organized the data so that they could see patterns to determine the typical name length for students in their class.

In the exploring phase, students created a table showing the data collected from the class about their names and the number of letters (see table 6.2). Mrs. Brown asked all students to first place the sticky note on which they had written the number of letters in their name on the front board to generate a set of class data. Then, to help the students investigate the concept of mean, the teacher had them build a tower with Unifix cubes representing the number of letters in their name. To continue exploring the data and to engage the whole class in a discussion about measures of center, the teacher asked who had the shortest and longest name in class and how this information could help her create a graphic representation. The students agreed that the persons with the shortest and longest names were Olga Topaz and Eugenia Estrella, respectively. The teacher created a line plot with the numbers from 9 to 15, as the students recommended (see fig. 6.1). Using the line plot, Mrs. Brown focused the discussion by asking students such questions as, "What is the mode of the number of letters?" Students could easily observe that the mode was 13. Next the teacher asked students to line up from smallest to largest number of letters to find the median. The students figured out that the median was 13 by looking at the number of Unifix cubes of the students who stood right in the middle of the line. To construct the mean, the students shared cubes with one another until they each had approximately the same number of cubes, which ended up being either 12 or 13. The teacher referred students to the line plot to have them reflect on what they were representing with their Unifix cubes.

In the summarizing phase of the lesson, the students were encouraged to make predictions based on the data in the line plot and asked to reflect

Table 6.2
*List of Students' Names in Mrs. Brown's Class**

Student's Name	No. of Letters
Esperanza Angel	14
Alfredo Durango	14
Eugenia Estrella	15
Angel Fortes	11
Cecilia Fortes	13
Aleman González	14
Edwin González	13
Roberto Guzman	13
Sofía Hernán	11
César López	10
Angela Lozano	12
Marcos Mares	11
Isela Mendoza	12
América Muñiz	12
Katrina Ozarta	13
Pacos Perales	12
Alba Rodríguez	13
Nicolas Sánchez	14
Adrian Sedillo	13
Arturo Sevilla	13
Olga Topaz	9
Neli Zapata	10

*Students' names are pseudonyms.

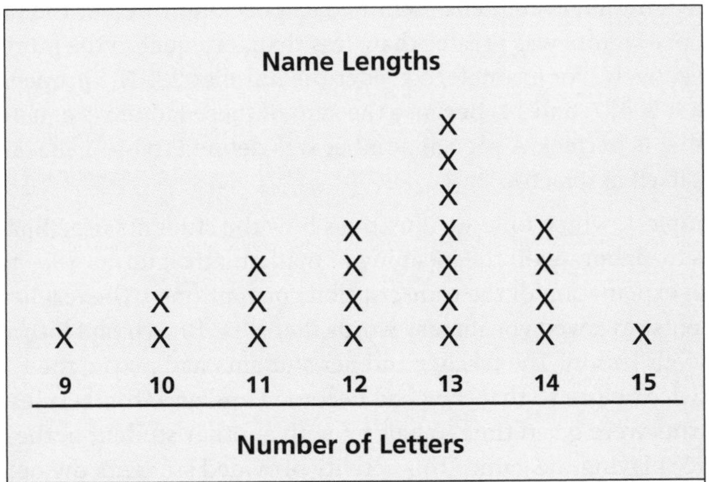

Name Lengths

				X		
				X		
				X		
			X	X	X	
		X	X	X	X	
	X	X	X	X	X	
X	X	X	X	X	X	X
9	**10**	**11**	**12**	**13**	**14**	**15**

Number of Letters

Fig. 6.1. Line plot

on how they had arranged their data with the Unifix cubes and in the line plot. Mrs. Brown reviewed the concepts of mean, median, and mode and ensured that students knew what effect adding a longer or shorter name would have on these three terms by asking them to think about how the new data would change (or not change) their solution. Students were asked to agree or disagree with the solutions and to explain their reasoning.

Using Cognates to Help ELLs Transfer Mathematical Meaning from Spanish to English

The Connected Mathematics Project materials used by students were written in English, so most of the lessons were taught in English. However, in some instances Mrs. Brown and her students used Spanish. In the lessons transcribed, one can observe that the patterns of the teacher's use of Spanish indicate that this choice was made to help students make meaning of mathematics terms and to explain mathematical problem-solving strategies using cognates. Cognates consist of words that are similar in spelling and meaning in two languages (e.g., *sum* and *suma*). An important point to note is that much mathematics and science terminology has roots that come from Greek or Latin; therefore, teachers should draw on this linguistic resource to support ELLs as they transfer meaning from Spanish to English (Cummins, as cited in Baker [2006]). In addition, research has shown that the use of cognates can be used to facilitate ELLs' development of English academic language (for examples in mathematics, see Celedón-Pattichis [2003]; Echeverría, Vogt, and Short [2004]; Genesee et al. [2005]; for practical ideas to implement in the classroom visit www.colorincolorado.org/teaching/vocabulary.php). Overall, the students often used cognates in Spanish when they needed to explain or expand their answers.

In a unit on number theory, students were introduced to such vocabulary as *factor, multiple, even* and *odd, proper factor, prime,* and *composite number*. In addition to these vocabulary words, students were exposed to the terms *abundant, deficient, perfect,* and *special*. Abundant, deficient, and perfect numbers could be identified by checking whether the sum of their proper factors was greater than, less than, or equal to the number itself, respectively. For example, consider the number 28. The proper factors of 28 are 1, 2, 4, 7, and 14. Because the sum of these factors is equal to 28, the number is perfect. A special number was defined to be "1" because it had only itself as a factor.

Example 1, which follows, illustrates how the students used Spanish cognates to elaborate on the meaning of mathematical terms. (See table 6.1 for an explanation of the transcription conventions.) The teacher and the students reviewed vocabulary words that Mrs. Brown had introduced in a previous lesson. The teacher and her students had played the Factor Game[3] twice before so that they had become familiar with the rules. Next, the students were given time to pair up with another student in the class to practice playing the game. This activity provided students the opportu-

3. For lessons and an online version of the Factor Game, see NCTM's Illuminations site, illuminations.nctm.org/LessonDetail.aspx?id=L620.

nity to use cognates as they attempted to make meaning of mathematics terminology within the context of the Factor Game. Teachers unfamiliar with the home language(s) of their ELLs might use a bilingual mathematics dictionary to search for such cognates.[4]

Example 1

1. *T:* ONE OF THESE CATEGORIES IS ABUNDANT. WHAT IS ABUNDANT?
2. *Ss:* **Abundante.**
   Abundant.
3. *T:* AND WHAT DOES THAT MEAN?
4. *Juany:* **Que tiene muchos factores.**
   That it has many factors.
5. *S:* **Deficiente.**
   Deficient.
6. *T:* WHAT? ((Not hearing clearly.))
7. *Juany:* It has a lot of factors.
8. *T:* WHAT ABOUT DEFICIENT?
9. *Ss:* **Deficiente.**
   Deficient.
10. *T:* AND WHAT DOES THAT MEAN?
11. *S:* **Ehh ... que no tiene mucho, tiene menos ...**
    Ehh ... that it doesn't have many, it has fewer ...
12. *T:* IT DOESN'T HAVE VERY ... MANY FACTORS. THE SUM OF ITS FACTORS, IN FACT, IS LESS THAN THE NUMBER ITSELF.

In lines 1 and 2 the teacher asked students to review the meaning of the word *abundant.* Students responded chorally in Spanish with *abundante* to find the corresponding word. In line 3, Mrs. Brown asked for the meaning of the word *abundant,* then Juany responded in Spanish to elaborate on its meaning (line 4). Juany repeated her response in English so that Mrs. Brown could hear her clearly (line 7).

Similarly, in line 8 Mrs. Brown asked students to explain the word *deficient.* In line 9, students responded in Spanish using the word *deficiente.* When Mrs. Brown asked for a specific meaning of the word (line 10), a student responded in Spanish to elaborate on the meaning of "deficient." In Example 1, only the students used Spanish to answer the teacher's questions. In responding, the students seemed to be using Spanish to activate the corresponding word first, then to elaborate on its meaning. In both cases (deficiente-deficient and abundante-abundant), Juany and other students used cognates, or similar words, to make meaning of vocabulary.

4. For an online glossary of mathematics terminology in Spanish, see www.mathnotes.com/aw_span_gloss.html and http://nw.pima.edu/dmeeks/spandict/.

Sometimes cognates can be easily confused by even the teacher, but such an occurrence can be a learning opportunity. For instance, the word *prime* was widely used throughout the unit and was used to make important points in several lessons. Mrs. Brown used *números primarios* as a translation of "prime numbers." During the first lesson of the unit, one student corrected the teacher, indicating that the correct term for "prime numbers" was *números primos*. Some students laughed because the only meaning they knew for *primos* translated to English as *cousins*. I was glad to see that the teacher was very open to students' suggestions. From that point on, Mrs. Brown used *números primos* for prime numbers.

Using Conceptually Based Games to Allow Students Opportunities to Communicate with Mathematical Language in a Nonthreatening Environment

Using the *Prime Time* unit (Lappan et al. 1996c), Mrs. Brown had many opportunities to allow students to discover strategies needed to win different games. This process involved the teacher's pushing for details in students' explanations using mathematical language to communicate their ideas. Although Mrs. Brown covered this unit at the beginning of the school year when most ELLs tend to go through a silent period (Baker 2006), the interactions between the teacher and the students show that students could engage in communicating their ideas when given the opportunity to do so in a nonthreatening way.

In example 2 below, Mrs. Brown used the Product Game (see figs. 6.2 and 6.3) to engage students in discovering strategies that would help them win[5]. The students had played the game twice previously.

Example 2

1. *T:* WHAT'S A GOOD THING TO DO IF YOU WANT TO WIN THE GAME? DID ANYBODY DISCOVER WAYS THAT HELP YOU TO WIN THE GAME?
2. *S1:* **Agarrar buenos números.**
   To get good numbers.
3. *T:* WHAT?
4. *S1:* **Agarrar buenos números.**
   To get good numbers.
   ((Teacher places Product Game on board.))
5. *T:* YEAH. AND WHAT ARE THE GOOD NUMBERS?
6. *S1:* **Cuarenta.**
   Forty.
7. *T:* WHY?
8. *S1:* **Porque puede seguir así** ((gestures with hand from left to right)) **para los lados y ...**
   Because you can continue like this to the sides and ...

5. For lessons and an online version of the Product Game, see NCTM's Illuminations site, illuminations.nctm.org/LessonDetail.aspx?ID=U100..

9. *T:* I DON'T UNDERSTAND.

10. *S2:* All of them are good.

11. *T:* EXPLAIN WHAT YOU'RE TALKING ABOUT.

12. *S1:* **Ese del medio.**
That one in the middle.

13. *T:* WHY SHOULD I PICK FORTY? WHY? WHY IS FORTY BETTER THAN SOME OTHER NUMBER?

14. *S1:* **Porque si agarra el veintiocho, se puede mover para arriba, para abajo.**
Because if you choose twenty-eight, you can move up, down.

15. *T:* **¿CUAL, CUARENTA?**
WHICH ONE, FORTY?

16. *S1:* **Veintiocho.**
Twenty-eight.

17. *T:* **OH, VEINTIOCHO.**
OH, TWENTY-EIGHT.
OK, OK. SO TWENTY-EIGHT HAS MORE POSSIBILITIES FOR DIRECTIONS.

18. *S1:* Yes.

19. *T:* SO ONE STRATEGY IS TO GET THE NUMBERS IN THE MIDDLE.
((Teacher writes this information on the board.))

Problem 2.1
Play the Product Game several times with a partner.
Look for interesting patterns and winning strategies.
Make notes of your observations.

Product Games Rules

1. Player A puts a paper clip on a number in the factor list. Player A does not mark a square on the product grid because only one factor has been marked: it takes two factors to mark a product.
2. Player B puts the other paper clip on any number in the factor list (including the same number marked by Player A) and then shades or covers the product of the two factors on the product grid.
3. Player A moves *either one* of the paper clips to another number and then shades or covers the new product.
4. Each player in turn moves a paper clip and marks a product. If a product is already marked, the player does not get a mark for that turn. The winner is the first player to mark four squares in a row—up and down, across, or diagonally.

Fig. 6.2. Rules for playing the Product Game.
Source: Lappan et al. (1996c); used with permission.

The Product Game

1	2	3	4	5	6
7	8	9	10	12	14
15	16	18	20	21	24
25	27	28	30	32	35
36	40	42	45	48	49
54	56	63	64	72	81

Factors:
1 2 3 4 5 6 7 8 9

Fig. 6.3. Board for playing the Product Game.
Source: Lappan et al. (1996c); used with permission.

In example 2, the teacher begins by posing an open-ended question about strategies that can help students win the Product Game. In lines 1–4, an exchange occurs between the teacher and a student who provides a general response ("To get good numbers"). In line 5, Mrs. Brown focuses on pushing for details by posing another open-ended question ("Yeah. And what are the good numbers?"). One student suggests the number 40; from lines 7 to 11 Mrs. Brown continues to ask for clarification of students' responses on why they would choose the number 40 and not some other number. In line 12 one student conjectures that choosing the number in the middle might be a strategy to win. The student supports his reasoning in line 14 ("Because if you choose 28, you can move up or down"). At the end, Mrs. Brown acknowledges the student's strategy by writing it on the board as one of the possible strategies to win.

To continue exploring which strategies might be helpful in winning, the teacher challenged students by asking them about good defensive strategies to stop an opponent from winning. One student explained that certain numbers should be avoided. Mrs. Brown asked for clarification by moving to more specific examples, such as, "Suppose your opponent needs the twenty-one. Where do you want to put your clip?" Most students responded, "On the three and the seven." The teacher continued this discussion by asking different "what if" questions substituting the numbers at the end of the question (e. g., "What if your opponent needs the twenty-eight?").

After students explored different moves in the Product Game, the teacher asked whether there was a way that they could prevent their opponent from getting the middle. One student responded "Yeah," to which

Mrs. Brown followed with, "How? Where can you put your clip that will prevent your opponent from getting in the middle?" The student responded, "On the one." Other students noted that choosing one was the best move because the highest number the opponent could get would be nine. Some students also noticed that if they had the opportunity to make the first move, they would choose one because this would give them the opportunity to get numbers in the middle of the game board. Mrs. Brown summarized the analysis of the Product Game by validating and revoicing students' responses and ideas on the board, as follows:

1. Get the numbers in the middle.
2. Avoid putting the clip on any number that your opponent *can* use.
3. If you go first, the best move is one.

This discussion allowed students different entry points to contribute how they were reasoning about factors, multiples, and products. By playing the game the students also developed computational fluency with multiplication facts, and the teacher was able to understand how students were using mathematical language to communicate their ideas.

In their review of the literature on motivation for achievement in mathematics, Middleton and Spanias (1999) state that the middle grades tend to be a crucial period when students consolidate their feelings toward mathematics and that "the findings of these studies suggest that the decline in positive attitudes toward mathematics can be explained in part as functions of lack of teacher supportiveness and classroom environment" (p. 67). Furthermore, "motivations toward mathematics are developed early, are highly stable over time, and are influenced greatly by teacher actions and attitudes" (p. 80). This example clearly shows that Mrs. Brown's actions involved creating a safe environment that promoted risk taking for all students in this inquiry-based classroom. The teacher validated what the students were explaining in their mathematical thinking, and how they were explaining it, to encourage them to understand mathematics.

Discussion and Implications

The teacher-student discourse patterns observed in Mrs. Brown's class provided information that was valuable in understanding the use of students' language and culture. Mrs. Brown served as an advocate for all her students and maintained high expectations in several ways. First, she welcomed the use of Spanish to facilitate learning for students in comprehending vocabulary that intersects in the daily use of English and the specific mathematical meaning (e.g., the terms *abundant, deficient,* and *perfect*). Worth noting here is that the development of mathematics vocabulary occurred in a context (i.e., the Product Game, Factor Game, or another theme) and not in disjointed events. In addition, the teacher set high expectations by not watering down either the mathematical content or the vocabulary that was presented in the CMP units and by pushing for details in students' explanations of their reasoning. By allowing the use of the students' native language, Mrs. Brown created different entry points for English language learners to expand explanations of their reasoning, even for students who would normally be reluctant to participate in mathematics classrooms. Second, the teacher made connections between her students' lives and the mathematics they were learning by affirming students' identities and experiences. Research shows that these practices are valuable in helping all students make connections with content-area learning (Echeverría, Vogt, and Short 2004). Thus, by integrating language-development strategies within mathematics lessons, teachers can successfully implement the NCTM Standards, an outcome that will benefit all students.

REFERENCES

Baker, Colin. *Foundations of Bilingual Education and Bilingualism.* 4th ed. Clevedon, Avon, England: Multilingual Matters, 2006.

Celedón-Pattichis, Sylvia. "Implementing Reform Curriculum: Voicing the Successes and Concerns of an ESL/Mathematics Teacher." Paper presented at the meeting of the National Association for Bilingual Education, Phoenix, Ariz., 2001.

———. "Constructing Meaning: Think-Aloud Protocols of ELLs on English and Spanish Word Problems." *Educators for Urban Minorities* 2, no. 2 (2003): 74–90.

Echeverria, Jana, Maryellen Vogt, and Deborah J. Short. *Making Content Comprehensible for English Learners: The SIOP Model.* New York: Pearson, 2004.

Fu, Danling. *My Trouble Is My English: Asian Students and the American Dream.* Portsmouth, N.H.: Heinemann, 1995.

Genesee, Fred, Kathryn Lindholm-Leary, William Saunders, and Donna Christian. "English Language Learners in U.S. Schools: An Overview of Research Findings." *Journal of Education for Students Placed at Risk* 10, no. 4 (2005): 363–86.

González, Norma, Luis C. Moll, and Cathy Amanti. *Funds of Knowledge: Theorizing Practices in Households, Communities, and Classrooms.* Mahwah, N.J.: Lawrence Erlbaum Associates, 2005.

Green, Judith L., and Cynthia Wallat. *Ethnography and Language in Educational Settings.* Norwood, N.J.: Ablex Publishing Corporation, 1981.

Heath, Shirley Brice. *Ways with Words: Language, Life, and Work in Communities and Classrooms.* New York: Cambridge University Press, 1983.

Khisty, Lena Licon. "Making Inequality: Issues of Language and Meanings in Mathematics Teaching with Hispanic Students." In *New Directions for Equity in Mathematics Education,* edited by Walter G. Secada, Elizabeth Fennema, and Lisa B. Adajian, pp. 279–97. New York: Cambridge University Press, 1995.

Khisty, Lena Licón, and Kathryn B. Chval. "Pedagogic Discourse and Equity in Mathematics: When Teachers' Talk Matters." *Mathematics Education Research Journal* 14, no. 3 (2002): 4–8.

Lappan, Glenda, James T. Fey, William M. Fitzgerald, Susan N. Friel, and Elizabeth Difanis Phillip. *Data about Us.* Palo Alto, Calif.: Dale Seymour Publications, 1996a.

———. *Getting to Know CMP.* Palo Alto, Calif.: Dale Seymour Publications, 1996b.

———. *Prime Time.* Palo Alto, Calif.: Dale Seymour Publications, 1996c.

Middleton, James A., and Photini A. Spanias. "Motivation for Achievement in Mathematics: Findings, Generalizations, and Criticisms of the Research." *Journal for Research in Mathematics Education* 30 (January 1999): 65–88.

Moschkovich, Judit N. "Supporting the Participation of English Language Learners in Mathematical Discussions." *For the Learning of Mathematics* 19, no.1 (1999): 11–19.

National Council of Teachers of Mathematics (NCTM). "Position Statement on Mathematics for Language Minority Students." Reston, Va.: NCTM, 1993.

———. *Principles and Standards for School Mathematics.* Reston, Va.: NCTM, 2000.

Tate, William F. *Access and Opportunity to Learn Are Not Accidents: Engineering Mathematical Progress in Your School.* Greensboro, N.C.: Southeast Eisenhower Regional Consortium for Mathematics and Science at SERVE, 2005.

Texas Education Agency (TEA). "Letter: Assessment Requirements for Students of Limited English Proficiency in the 1995–1996 State Testing Program." Austin, Tex.: TEA, 1996.

Thomas, Wayne P., and Virginia Collier. *School Effectiveness for Language Minority Students.* Washington, D.C.: National Clearinghouse for Bilingual Education, 1997.

Wells, Gordon. "The Negotiation of Meaning: Talking and Learning at Home and at School." In *Home and School: Early Language and Reading,* edited by Bryant Fillion, Carolyn N. Hedly, and Emily C. DiMartino, pp. 3–25. Norwood, N.J.: Ablex Publishing Corporation, 1987.

7

Supporting Middle School Students with Learning Disabilities in the Mathematics Classroom

Kristin K. Stang

PRINCIPLES and Standards for Mathematics (NCTM 2000) challenges that all students should be exposed to "a rich and integrated treatment of mathematics content" (p. 213). For this outcome to be realized, students with learning disabilities should be included in general education mathematics instruction whenever appropriate. Furner, Yahya, and Duffy (2005) noted that "equity in mathematics instruction requires teachers to provide accommodations so that everyone in the class can learn mathematics" (p. 22). In addition, as many school districts are requiring that all students pass algebra (Gagnon and Maccini 2001), increasingly greater numbers of students with special needs are being educated in general education mathematics classrooms. All these requirements result in additional responsibilities for the general education teacher of mathematics who must provide specific supports for these students (DeSimone and Parmar 2006).

Decisions regarding services for students with learning disabilities are made on the basis of individual needs and legal qualification criteria as well as the impact of a disability on participation in each content area (IDEIA 2004). With the increasing demands placed on students and schools in terms of mathematics course-taking and performance on state tests, many students with learning disabilities are being educated in the general mathematics classroom. Furthermore, although approximately 6 percent of students are estimated to have a specific learning disability in mathematics (Fleischner and Manheimer 1997), mathematics performance can be also affected by other learning disabilities (LD), including disabilities in reading, writing, and oral language, as well as by attention deficit–hyperactivity disorder (ADHD). This finding means that many more than 6 percent of students may struggle with mathematics because of a disability and still be included in the general education classroom. Thus the general education mathematics teacher must be aware of two important considerations—(1) how different disabilities may affect students' learning of mathematics and (2) the many strategies and resources available to help them provide accommodations that make mathematics accessible to all students.

With the increasing demands placed on students and schools in terms of mathematics course-taking and performance on state tests, many students with learning disabilities are being educated in the general mathematics classroom.

General Accommodations and Modifications

The Individualized Education Program (IEP) provides students with learning disabilities specific accommodations and, if necessary, modifications that must take place in any classroom in which they are educated. Accommodations involve changing how a student takes in information or tells teachers what they know; they may include a variety of both instructional and assessment adaptations. An important point to note is that accommodations do not involve changing the expected learning outcomes. Modifications actually change the content taught, by changing what is expected for the student to learn.

In mathematics the most obvious instructional accommodation, perhaps, is the use of a times table or a calculator. However, being afforded that accommodation by his or her IEP does not mean that a student has the knowledge to use the tool efficiently. Middle school students need training to use tools and manipulatives effectively in your classroom. For example, just handing a student a calculator will not necessarily result in an academic benefit. Teachers need to model calculator use and teach students how to use the tool. One way to do so would be by including instruction in calculator use while leading the class through a sample problem. Another way would be through an activity in which students can discover various ways to solve a problem using the tool, with a discussion of the problem-solving activity after the students' learning and discovery have occurred.

Other simple accommodations exist that benefit students with a variety of needs in the middle school mathematics classroom. These accommodations are all inexpensive and time efficient, and they can be used effectively in middle school inclusive classroom settings. For example, students with visual or physical impairments, ADHD, or a written-language disorder may make computational errors due to difficulty with number alignment. Graph or grid paper can be adapted by using a photocopy machine until each box is the size of a student's handwritten number, thus providing a guide for number alignment. Making multiple copies, storing them in a folder, and making it a student's responsibility to take the paper when needed can add in support for students' self-determination skills as well. Similarly, lined notebook paper can be turned horizontally so that the lines create columns, thus offering an additional guide for number alignment. Figures 7.1 and 7.2 show examples of each of these accommodations. Additionally, a three-ring binder can be turned horizontally so that the rings are toward the back of the desk to create a slant board. Students with disabilities that affect visual processing may benefit from writing their work on the binder, thus not looking different from their peers.

Many middle school teachers use grouping for cooperative learning. Being integrated in groups across the classroom is important for students with learning disabilities as well as students with other diverse needs, such as language differences. Having a single group composed only of students with special needs creates a segregated environment in what is supposed

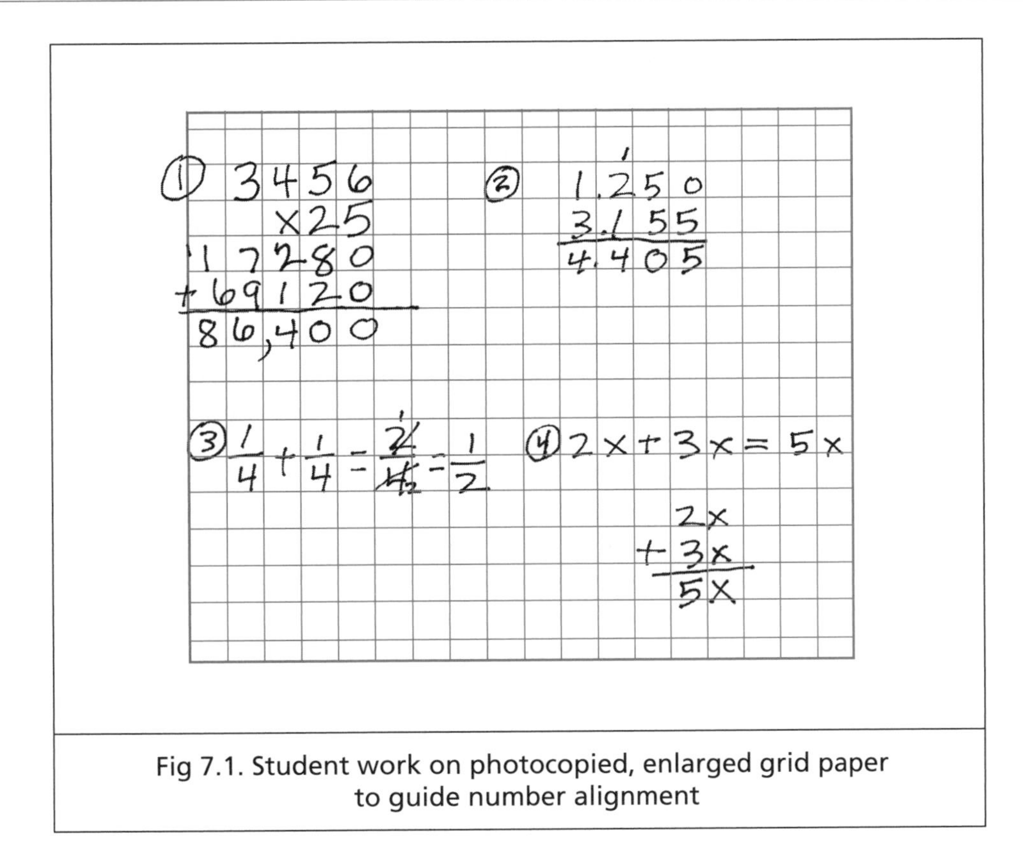

Fig 7.1. Student work on photocopied, enlarged grid paper to guide number alignment

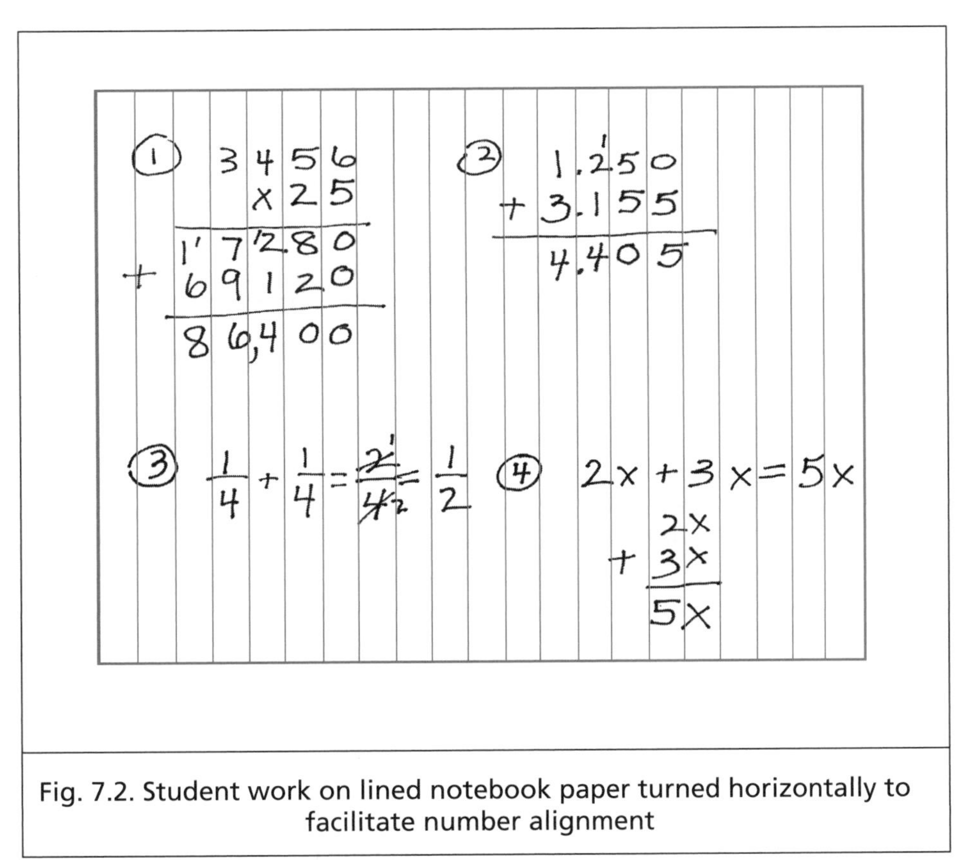

Fig. 7.2. Student work on lined notebook paper turned horizontally to facilitate number alignment

to be an inclusion setting. If you do use grouping in your classroom, an important consideration is to assign roles in ways that allow each student to bring some strength to the cooperative task (Cohen 1994). For example, roles could be assigned so that a student with a written language disability is assigned the job of facilitator. Preplanning the groups and roles for this type of instructional activity is an easy way to support diverse learners successfully.

In addition to accommodations for instruction, teachers may need to make accommodations for assessment. Assessment accommodations may include accepting oral responses instead of, or in addition to, written responses. Extended time for tests is a frequently assigned accommodation but should be used only when it is necessary. As a wise student once said, "Extended time does not mean extended knowledge." But for some students additional time may be beneficial if they have a slow reading or writing pace that makes timed testing particularly difficult. Some students may need to have specific test items read aloud. If you do not have a paraprofessional or special education teacher in your classroom, arrangements should be made so that any student needing a read-aloud test can receive that support elsewhere.

Different from accommodations, *modifications* traditionally occur for students with more significant learning disabilities who have been determined not to be learning grade-level content, even if they are learning the same topic. In general, modifications are considered those instances in which the content of the lesson is altered in such a way that the student is working toward a different standard. Modifications are always done in consultation with a student's special education teacher and must be clearly documented in the student's IEP. The majority of students with learning disabilities, however, are best served by teachers' use of accommodations that give them opportunities to achieve grade-level content standards.

The Importance of Opportunities to Focus on Mathematical Concepts and Connections

NCTM (2000) states that during the middle grades, "students will solidify conceptions about themselves as learners of mathematics" (p. 210). This outcome becomes even more important when we consider the fact that students with learning disabilities may lose motivation and face a decline in attitude toward school as they transition from elementary school to high school (Anderman 1998), or may struggle with self-efficacy because of previous failures in mathematics (Jones, Wilson, and Bhojwani 1997). Woodward and Montague (2002) have noted that students with LD should not spend "inordinate" time working on computational-skill mastery and instead should focus on developing their skills of problem solving and analysis. Likewise, Cawley (2002) suggests that students with learning disabilities need instruction that focuses not only on "doing" mathematics but on "knowing about" mathematics. Shifting the focus in such a way helps students who may struggle with mental computation, for example, to gain access to, and make sense of, mathematical concepts and connections and can, in turn, increase their interest and motivation in mathematics.

In my middle school classroom, I had many visual supports that our program purchased for teaching students with learning disabilities about the addition and subtraction of fractions. But one of the most effective tools I had was something inexpensive that I made myself. Using lightweight cardboard from gift boxes, I created fraction kits. When we worked with fractions, each student had at her or his desk a kit that contained pieces in the form of either a circular pie or a rectangular strip. Each individual piece was clearly labeled on the front with its fraction value relative to the whole, with several units represented (halves, thirds, fourths, fifths, sixths, and so on). When we began to discuss equivalent fractions or the idea of adding or subtracting fractions, students first tried to solve the problems using their kits. For example, students could find out how many 1/4 pieces fit into the whole strip or pie, or explore how many sixteenths fit into a quarter. Throughout the year, I had students write equivalent fractions on the back of each piece so that by the end of the term, the whole pie or strip had, for example, 1/1 = 2/2 = 3/3 = 4/4 or 1/2 = 2/4 = 3/6 = 4/8 written on the back for reference. As students developed stronger conceptual understanding of this procedure, many stopped using the manipulatives altogether, whereas others looked at the equivalent fraction list on the back of the piece only to solve the assigned problems. A great resource for the use of visual models to teach students about fractions is found at NCTM's Illuminations Web site, illuminations.nctm.org/ActivityDetail.aspx?id=11.

Although the research base for the specific instruction required for students with learning disabilities in mathematics may not be strong enough to determine a particular list of "best strategies" (Jones, Wilson, and Bhojwani 1997), recent research has contributed to our ever-increasing knowledge of effective instruction for these students. Some of the difficulty in bringing research to practice may result from the unique impact of disability on the individual student.

One area of agreement has to do with the importance of structure and organization for students with learning disabilities. Jones, Wilson and Bhojwani (1997) contend that students with LD will experience success only in a mathematics classroom in which the teacher delivers high-quality instruction that is well-organized and clearly presented. Teachers should also allow students with learning disabilities to participate in problem solving through experiences in guided practice before requiring them to complete the work in independent practice (Witzel, Smith, and Brownell 2001). Along with this recommendation, research has demonstrated the importance of identifying in advance the prerequisite skills students need to solve a mathematics problem so as to determine points at which individualized instruction for students with learning disabilities may need to occur (Gagnon and Maccini 2001). Furthermore, research recommends that teachers "dialogue" among students about each step of a problem so that the process of error analysis can take place both as a means to support students' self-monitoring of their learning and as a way to make the teacher

A growing body of research shows that students with learning disabilities benefit from "hands-on learning," a unified curriculum, and mathematics instruction that contains "higher-order reasoning and critical-thinking skills."

aware of topics that may need to be retaught (Witzel, Smith, and Brownell 2001).

When it comes to specific learning activities, a growing body of research shows that students with learning disabilities benefit from "hands-on learning," a unified curriculum, and mathematics instruction that contains "higher-order reasoning and critical-thinking skills" (Maccini and Gagnon 2000). Fleischner and Manheimer (1997) assert that teachers need to teach mathematical concepts by moving from the concrete to the abstract. Witzel, Smith, and Brownell (2001) suggest that moving instruction from concrete to abstract scenarios will help students with learning disabilities better learn algebra. This approach is further supported by the work of Witzel, Mercer, and Miller (2003), who found that students with learning disabilities who experienced concrete-to-representational-to-abstract (CRA) algebra instruction outperformed matched peers who did not receive such instruction. The K–8 Access Center has an excellent description of CRA, tools for using CRA in your classroom , and online resources describing this strategy (www.k8accesscenter.org/training_resources/CRA_Instructional_Approach.asp). This Web site not only provides information on the model but also gives examples for how to use it in your classroom and offers additional resources to review.

Professional Collaboration to Support Students' Learning

General educators do not need to meet the needs of students with learning disabilities alone. In fact, DeSimone and Parmar (2006) found professional collaboration to be a "valuable resource" for general educators as they successfully taught mathematics to students with learning disabilities in their classrooms. Collaboration does not occur just with special educators. General education teachers have reported that administrative support was crucial to their success as they took steps to include students with learning disabilities in their middle school mathematics classrooms (DeSimone and Parmar 2006). Training and support beyond the initial teacher preparation is also important. Teachers with access to professional development opportunities specific to teaching mathematics in an inclusion setting report feeling better prepared to support students with learning disabilities in their classrooms (DeSimone and Parmar).

Maccini and Gagnon (2006) reported that general educators used significantly fewer "recommended" instructional practices in teaching mathematics to students with learning disabilities than did special education teachers. They suggested that the best way to merge the content strengths of general educators and the individualized instructional strengths of the special educators is through collaboration. One collaborative teaching model frequently used in the middle-level classrooms is the coteaching model, in which two expert teachers (one special education and one general education) coteach or team teach a course or unit (Cook and Friend 1995; Fennick and Liddy 2001; Gerber and Popp 2000). Coteaching, also known as collaborative teaching or cooperative teaching, is best illustrated as the approach in which two education professionals share responsibilities for instruction. Coteaching is known to be an effective method for successfully including students with learning disabilities in general education classrooms (Fennick 2001). Instructional models for coteaching may vary (Cook and Friend 1995; Vaughn, Schumm, and Arguelles 1997; Walsh and Jones 2004), but all models emphasize the importance of the collaborative partnership and the communication and flexibility required to adjust instructional delivery on the basis of knowledge of both students and curriculum. Studies have shown that through the use of coteaching for academic support, students with special needs experience increased self-concept and self-esteem as well as increased general academic outcomes (Dieker 2001; Walsh and Jones 2004).

Administrative support is crucial to the success of coteaching (Fennick 2001; Gerber and Popp 2000; Stang and Capp 2004), and this support includes administrative involvement in special education (Cook and Friend 1995; Walther-Thomas 1997). If specific time for the general educator to coplan with the special education teacher is not allocated, individualized instruction by the special educator may never occur (Magiera et al. 2005). Likewise, researchers also suggest that common planning time for the teaching team plays an important role in a positive coteaching experience for both students and teachers (Cook and Friend 1995; Dieker 2001; Murawski and Dieker 2004; Vaughn, Schumm, and Arguelles 1997).

Middle School Mathematics and Coteaching

Ideally, a coteaching relationship in a middle school classroom would include a general educator as the expert on content and a special educator as the expert on individualized instruction and accommodations (Magiera et al. 2005). However, concerns about the implementation of coteaching in mathematics classrooms exist. Magiera and her colleagues (2005) discovered that too often in secondary school mathematics classrooms, the general education teacher and special education teacher were not really coteaching, because the special educator merely served as an assistant to the classroom teacher instead of a teaching partner. Why is this arrangement occurring?

In middle and high school mathematics classrooms, the general education teacher is trained to be a content expert, and few general education teachers report that their preservice training helped them with strategies for the successful inclusion of students with learning disabilities (DeSimone and Parmar 2006). The importance of having access to collaboration with a special education teacher is underscored by research showing that middle school mathematics teachers report often feeling uncomfortable supporting students with a learning disability even though they are typically the primary mathematics instructor for these children (DeSimone and Parmar 2006).

The importance of having access to collaboration with a special education teacher is underscored by research showing that middle school mathematics teachers report often feeling uncomfortable supporting students with a learning disability even though they are typically the primary mathematics instructor for these children.

Conclusions

With the reform movement in mathematics, "it is hoped that new directions in mathematics education will help to move students with learning disabilities out of a narrow and highly procedural set of experiences closer to the kind of mathematical instruction that is valued today" (Woodward and Montague 2002, p. 98). This goal is a challenge to teachers to provide students with learning disabilities access to learning rich mathematics content. Among the strategies we know help toward this end are offering students opportunities to work cooperatively with peers in solving mathematics problems and structuring lessons that allow students to move from concrete to abstract mathematical representations. In these ways, middle school mathematics can be for *all* students, including those with learning disabilities.

When working with students with learning disabilities in the middle school mathematics classroom, the teacher must fully understand the identified needs of the student, including any required accommodations or modifications.

Additionally, the value of mathematics teachers' collaborating with their special education colleagues cannot be overemphasized. When working with students with learning disabilities in the middle school mathematics classroom, the teacher must fully understand the identified needs of the student, including any required accommodations or modifications. Instruction may need to be individualized for some of these students. Collaboration with the special educator is the best way for the mathematics teacher to gain specific information about what has worked for those individual students in the past, as well as what required accommodations or modifications are called for by their IEP. Ultimately, students with learning disabilities are best served by efforts made to leverage the collective professional expertise in your school's staff.

REFERENCES

Anderman, Eric M. "The Middle School Experience: Effects on the Math and Science Achievement of Adolescents with LD." *Journal of Learning Disabilities* 31, no. 2 (1998): 128–38.

Cawley, John F. "Mathematics Interventions and Students with High-Incident Disabilities." *Remedial and Special Education* 23, no. 1 (2002): 2–6.

Cohen, Elizabeth G. *Designing Group Work: Strategies for the Heterogeneous Classroom.* 2d ed. New York: Teachers College Press, 1994.

Cook, Lynne, and Marilyn Friend. "Coteaching: Guidelines for Creating Effective Practices." *Focus on Exceptional Children* 28, no. 3 (1995): 1–16.

DeSimone, Janet R., and Rene S. Parmer. "Middle School Mathematics Teachers' Beliefs about Inclusion of Students with Learning Disabilities." *Learning Disabilities Research and Practice* 21, no. 2 (2006): 98–110.

Dieker, Lisa A. "What Are the Characteristics of 'Effective' Middle and High School Cotaught Teams for Students with Disabilities?" *Preventing School Failure* 46 (2001): 14–23.

Fennick, Ellen. "Coteaching: An Inclusive Curriculum for Transition." *Teaching Exceptional Children* 33, no. 6 (2001): 61–66.

Fennick, Ellen, and Deana Liddy. "Responsibilities and Preparation for Collaborative Teaching: Coteachers' Perspectives." *Teacher Education and Special Education* 24, no. 3 (2001): 229–40.

Fleischner, Jeanette E., and Maris A. Manheimer. "Math Interventions for Students with Learning Disabilities: Myths and Realities." *School Psychology Review* 26, no. 3 (1997): 397–418.

Furner, Joseph M., Noorchaya Yahya, and Mary Lou Duffy. "20 Ways to Teach Mathematics: Strategies to Reach All Students." *Intervention in School and Clinic* 41, no. 1 (2005): 16–23.

Gagnon, Joseph C., and Paul Maccini. "Preparing Students with Disabilities for Algebra." *Teaching Exceptional Children* 34, no. 1 (2001): 8–15.

Gerber, Paul J., and Patricia A. Popp. "Making Collaborative Teaching More Effective for Academically Able Students: Recommendations for Implementation and Training." *Learning Disability Quarterly* 23 (2000): 229–35.

Individuals with Disabilities Education Improvement Act (IDEIA) *of 2004*. Public Law 108–446, *U. S. Statutes at Large* 118 (2004): 2647.

Jones, Eric D., Rich Wilson, and Shalini Bhojwani. "Mathematics Instruction for Secondary Students with Learning Disabilities." *Journal of Learning Disabilities* 30, no. 2 (1997): 151–63.

Maccini, Paul, and Jospeh C. Gagnon. "Best Practices for Teaching Mathematics to Secondary Students with Special Needs." *Focus on Exceptional Children* 32, no. 5 (2000): 1–22.

————. "Mathematics Instructional Practices and Assessment Accommodations by Secondary Special and General Educators." *Exceptional Children* 72, no. 2 (2006): 217–34.

Magiera, Kathleen, Cynthia Smith, Naomi Zigmond, and Kelli Gerbaurer. "Benefits of Coteaching in Secondary Mathematics Classes." *Teaching Exceptional Children* 37, no. 3 (2005): 20–24.

Murawski, Wendy W., and Lisa A. Dieker. "Tips and Strategies for Coteaching at the Secondary Level." *Teaching Exceptional Children* 5 (2004): 52–58.

National Council of Teachers of Mathematics (NCTM). *Principles and Standards for School Mathematics.* Reston, Va.: NCTM, 2000.

Stang, Kristin K., and Gordon P. Capp. "Coteaching: Collaboration at the Middle Level." *Academic Exchange Quarterly* 8, no. 3 (2004): 228–32.

Vaughn, Sharon, Jean S. Schumm, and Maria E. Arguelles. "The ABCDEs of Coteaching." *Teaching Exceptional Children* 30 (1997): 4–10.

Walsh James W., and Barbara Jones. "New Models of Cooperative Teaching." *Teaching Exceptional Children* 36, no. 5 (2004): 14–20.

Walther-Thomas, Christine. "Coteaching Experiences: The Benefits and Problems That Teachers and Principals Report over Time." *Journal of Learning Disabilities* 30 (1997): 395–407.

Witzel, Bradley S., Stephen W. Smith, and Mary T. Brownell. "How Can I Help Students with Learning Disabilities Learn Algebra?" *Intervention in School and Clinic* 37, no. 2 (2001): 101–4.

Witzel, Bradley S., Cecil D. Mercer, and M. David Mille. "Teaching Algebra to Students with Learning Difficulties: An Investigation of an Explicit Instruction Model." *Learning Disabilities Research and Practice* 18, no. 2 (2003): 121–31.

Woodward, John, and Marjorie Montague. "Meeting the Challenge of Mathematics Reform for Students with LD." *Journal of Special Education* 32, no. 2 (2002): 89–101.

8

Self-Differentiating in Inclusion Classrooms: Opportunities to Learn

Signe E. Kastberg
Wendy Otoupal-Hylton
Sherri Farmer

THE INCLUSION of students with special education labels has encouraged teachers to reexamine traditional practices in, and adopt new approaches to, supporting the learning of all children (Williams and Baxter 1996; Woodward and Montague 2002). In this article we explore (1) the work of two middle school students who carry special education labels and (2) the practice of their mathematics teacher. The students' work challenged the teacher's understanding of mathematics and triggered her instinct to preserve the essential trust she had developed with the students. We share the teacher's approach to the students' solution and the factors that she suggested affected her judgment. Finally, we explore the potential of the students' solution that we viewed as an opportunity for our own learning and that resulted in the development of a problem for further whole-class investigation.

Building Understandings of Area and Perimeter: Exploring a Dog's Life

In the spring of 2005 the authors of this article had the unique opportunity to explore the contributions of students with special education labels to their mathematics classes. We worked together for five months in Wendy's multiage, multigrade inclusion classroom and spent additional time working together to make sense of what we had seen. In our roles as a research team, Signe coordinated the research effort and engaged in the classroom as a participant observer, Sherri was an undergraduate researcher and engaged in the classroom as a participant observer, and Wendy was the middle school mathematics teacher and researcher. Signe and Wendy had known each other since the spring of 2003, had planned lessons together, had observed and critiqued each other's teaching, and had begun writing together. Sherri was new to the team and as such provided a unique perspective neither Signe nor Wendy had captured.

Data collected in the classroom included observations of one pair of students who carried special education labels. Penny, a very social sixth grader, was a wonderfully outgoing girl with a personal strength and desire to interact with others. She had transferred to the school at the beginning of sixth grade and was thoroughly engaged in making new friends. Stacey, a shy seventh grader, was reserved and emotionally strong. Since she had transferred to the school at the beginning of her sixth-grade year, she had served as an academic role model for Penny. In turn Penny had served as a social role model for Stacey. Wendy had not paired the two girls. Instead they had formed a bond that tapped the strengths of each girl. Stacey was organized and diligent yet quiet and reserved. Penny was talkative and interactive yet disorganized and distracted. Penny often played the role of the spokesperson for the two, whereas Stacey organized their written work and summarized findings from their explorations.

Wendy's response to the challenge of supporting the development of students from a vast array of grade levels was to adopt an inquiry-based approach. She believed that this approach would allow students to "meet the problem" at their existing academic and developmental levels. In our discussions about her approach, we began to call students' behavior in an inquiry-based classroom *self-differentiating*. Self-differentiating contrasts with differentiated instruction in that the students interpret instruction and make assumptions that are unexpected and lead to the development of unique strategies and solutions. The assumption that students can and do interpret instruction and tasks stems from our perspective on children as sense makers (von Glasersfeld 1995). In this view, the tasks alone do not carry meaning or challenges. Instead, a student's interpretation of the words and intent of the task using her or his own existing understanding makes a task problematic. In an inquiry-based classroom, in which the teacher supports the development of autonomy, students' interpretations of tasks are not assumed to be fixed; rather, the teacher embraces the diversity of approaches and solutions that emerge from students' differentiated interpretations, strategies, and solutions. The role of the teacher is to observe and gather evidence of students' thinking as she or he prepares to engage the students in a whole-class discussion of what can be a diverse collection of approaches to a problem.

In an inquiry-based classroom, in which the teacher supports the development of autonomy, students' interpretations of tasks are not assumed to be fixed; rather, the teacher embraces the diversity of approaches and solutions that emerge from students' differentiated interpretations, strategies, and solutions.

In inclusion classrooms the teacher typically has in mind mathematical goals as well as affective and social goals. In Wendy's class she had broad mathematical objectives, such as the development of content and process as described in the 6–8 grade band in *Principles and Standards for School Mathematics* (National Council of Teachers of Mathematics [NCTM] 2000). In addition Wendy also supported goals that she and her students had established for their social and emotional achievement. This attention to the whole child stemmed from the environment of the school, in which the talents of all children and their future contributions to society were highly prized. Wendy's approach to the needs of the whole child included the development of a community of learners (Cobb, Wood, and Yackel 1990). Wendy described her class and the approaches she used in the following manner:

> We establish classroom norms, that we call "procedures," at the beginning of the year. Each class consists of students academically labeled as sixth, seventh, and eighth grade, leaving

> the diversity of mathematical understanding between basic number recognition and more advanced algebraic reasoning. As a result of this extremely diverse population, the efforts to build community are essential for classroom learning to be effective. Because of the diversity, we always read aloud the problem for the day and check both for understanding of the context and the expected behavior, what they are trying to produce. The students are then allowed time to explore the variety of potential strategies and solutions while music is used for volume control ("If you can't hear the music, you're too loud"). I wander around, checking for understanding and applied effort, and only redirect [an exploration] when the group has not self-corrected within a few minutes. (Excerpt from Wendy's written reflection, May 23, 2005)

Students were free to form groups and work in the hall or the classroom as they explored a problem. An essential element of these relationships seemed to be a mutual respect in which autonomy was developed and each student came to view himself or herself as important to the other members of the class.

The development of such an environment leaves the teacher free to use a single problem to meet the needs of all students. The teacher trusts that the students will interpret the problem using their existing understandings and that those interpretations will be reflected in their solutions. The teacher can then draw on the sense making of the students when conducting a whole-class discussion of the mathematics used. If a student self-differentiated a problem, Wendy knew that the student's strategies, assumptions, and feelings could provide opportunities for her own learning and that of the other students. To illustrate how students self-differentiated by interpreting a problem differently than the teacher intended, we share the following episode from Sherri's observation notes. During the lesson the students were asked to "create" a dog pen. The mathematical objective of the lesson was to explore relationships between perimeter and area of a rectangle; however, in the inquiry-based classroom the initial objective must be set or modified if students' strategies and solutions suggest an opportunity to explore significant mathematics not initially planned for. An excerpt from the text including the problem the students were asked to solve follows; Sherri's field notes that include Stacey and Penny's approach to the problem are then presented.

The teacher trusts that the students will interpret the problem using their existing understandings and that those interpretations will be reflected in their solutions.

> Suppose you wanted to help a friend build a rectangular pen for her dog, Shane. You have 24 meters of fencing, in 1-meter lengths, to build the pen. Which rectangular shape would be the best for Shane? (Lappan et al. 2002, p. 36)

Sherri's notes

Stacey [S] and Penny [P] talked about the shape of the dog pen.

S: I have a dog, and she likes to play.

P: Yeah, I know your dog.

S: She usually runs along the fence barking at stuff on the other side. But when we play, we play by her house.

P: So what shape would be best?

S: Well, we need a small space to put the dog house in. That can be her space for play and rest.

P: But the question says the dog needs running room.

S: *Then we just make a bigger area ... here ... for her to run in.*

Sherri's notes: The small pen at the top was 2 meters by 3 meters. The bottom part of the pen was 6 meters by 3 meters. The total perimeter of this "pen" is 24 meters (see fig. 8.1).

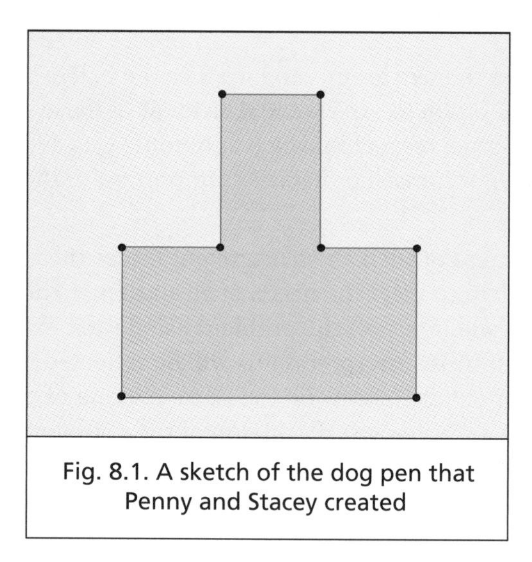

Fig. 8.1. A sketch of the dog pen that Penny and Stacey created

Penny and Stacey successfully generated a pen with a perimeter of 24 meters, as was required in the problem, but in addition their dog pen had an area of 24 square meters. The girls had solved "the problem" in the sense that they had differentiated the task by generating a solution that made sense to them using their understanding of the problem, of the needs of a dog, and of mathematics. Upon observing this solution, it was up to Wendy whether to include it when supporting a whole-class discussion of various student solutions, many of which included rectangles, to generate opportunities for all students to learn.

Judgment Calls "on the Fly"

At the conclusion of the group investigation time, Wendy asked different groups to present their solutions and used those solutions to facilitate a discussion of the mathematics they contained. In Wendy's class the expectation was that all children would present solutions in class but that Wendy would determine the order of presenters. She called her approach to ordering presenters an "on the fly judgment." Although this description sounds haphazard, Wendy's process was not. In her conversations with different groups of children during the investigation of a problem, she analyzed the approaches used so that she could make choices about solutions and strategies to highlight. She was attentive to the idea that "there is never just one strategy to solve a problem," and she was interested in having a diversity of presenters share an array of solutions, as long as they helped students explore the objective of the lesson. Wendy's expectation was that all students would spontaneously share or be invited to share their thinking during the semester. Her desire to have many strategies shared and discussed and her sensitivity to the time remaining for whole-class discussion during a lesson were additional factors that she juggled as she made judgments "on the fly."

As Wendy walked around the room listening to the students and observing their explorations, she noticed that Penny and Stacey had not drawn a rectangle. Instead they had used twenty-four 1-by-1 paper squares to create their dog pen. Wendy quickly decided not to include Penny and Stacey's solution in the whole-class discussion, and suggested to the girls that their answer "was not a rectangle" and so did not meet the conditions of the problem. Although at first glance this observation may seem harsh, Wendy's response was not simply a reaction to the students' solution. Instead several important factors went into Wendy's decision to redirect the students during their investigation: trust, expectations, and mathematics.

Wendy worked hard to build trust in the classroom community, but of crucial importance to her was that she should get to know each student and earn his or her trust. Trust was essential in that all students were expected to explore problems, create solutions, present findings, and discuss ideas. In the discussion of their ideas, all students had to be prepared to engage—to defend and, at times, to confront the limitations of their solutions. Limitations in solutions came in many forms, including failure to meet the criteria given in the problem statement. Wendy asserted that all children, regardless of label, needed to have opportunities to learn mathematics by communicating their thinking and interpreting the thinking of others. In her evaluation of Penny and Stacey's solution, Wendy identified what she viewed as a flaw. In discussing her decision to point this flaw out to them, she explained that if she as the teacher did not find a way to communicate or provoke a realization of the flaw, she would be implying that she expected less of them than she did of other students. For Wendy the mathematical goal of the lesson was the exploration of connections between area and fixed perimeter of *rectangles*.

Trust was essential in that all students were expected to explore problems, create solutions, present findings, and discuss ideas.

Although these two students did not approach the problem in same way as many of their peers, they did confront the challenge of exploring relationships between area and perimeter, a broader mathematical goal for the course. They did understand as they manipulated the paper squares that the perimeter would not be fixed although the area would be so. In addition, they found an area that was actually sufficient for both a dog run and a dog pen. Their approach met a broader mathematical objective, understanding relationships between area and perimeter, even though it failed to explore relationships between fixed perimeter and area. Wendy's "judgment" made "on the fly" with knowledge of the two students, a relationship built on trust and high expectations, and a mathematical goal in mind made sense for her during the lesson but may represent a missed opportunity, something we discuss in the next section.

In inquiry-based classrooms teachers must make many quick decisions about how to structure whole-class discussions.

In inquiry-based classrooms teachers must make many quick decisions about how to structure whole-class discussions. A teacher may have many ideas or even some experience with strategies that students might use or solutions they might generate, but an element of uncertainty always exists about the directions that could emerge during a discussion of students' work. As Wendy and Signe discussed the potential in Penny and Stacey's solution, they realized that including the solution felt risky to Wendy in two related ways. Wendy described feeling unprepared to "take it [the girls' solution] down a path that supported their finding to their peers on an intellectual basis." Without understanding the potential of the girls' solution, Wendy thought that she would be unable to support a whole-class discussion that would result in peers' viewing the girls' solution as meaningful. For Wendy, her own difficulty recognizing the mathematical potential of the solution became an impediment to including it in the whole-class discussion and suggested to her a very real danger of unintentionally positioning Penny and Stacey as less able than their peers.

An Alternative Ending: The Potential of Penny and Stacey's Solution

Although the solution Penny and Stacey generated did not meet the criteria in the problem statement, we realized the power of their solution as we tried to find other solutions that met the girls' much more realistic criteria for a dog pen. Penny and Stacey used their experience with Stacey's dog as the basis for their design. The pen needed to include space for the dog to run and space for a dog house. The fence should be used to enclose both the house and the play area. These conditions, drawn from the girls' solution, did, indeed, have the potential to support the investigation of significant mathematics—related to the objectives of the lesson—while meeting the litmus test for "realistic" that was set up by the girls' assumptions. Perhaps as a result of their experiences exploring spaces with fixed area in the previous investigation, the girls used twenty-four 1-by-1 paper squares to create their model. The use of the squares did not ensure that the generated shape would have a perimeter of 24 "meters," and yet the dog pen the girls created did have a perimeter of 24 paper units (which represented meters). As posed, the original task had given a fixed perimeter; however, the girls had solved the problem using a fixed area and had meet the conditions for perimeter. To explore the mathematical potential of the girls' solution, we posed the following question that Wendy might have used either in the whole-class discussion or as a follow-up during the next lesson.

> In the original problem you were asked to create a rectangular dog pen with 24 meters of fencing in 1-meter lengths. Penny and Stacey created their pen to meet the needs of Stacey's dog, who likes to play and run but also likes to sleep in his house. The pen they created is made from two adjoin-

ing rectangles whose total area is 24 square meters and is enclosed by 24 meters of fencing. How many pens can we make using adjoining rectangles, whose total area is 24 square meters, and that can be enclosed using exactly 24 meters of fencing in 1-meter lengths?

As we considered this problem we realized that the girls, using two adjoining rectangles, had identified the dog pen that enclosed the maximum area for the dog to play (see fig.8.2).

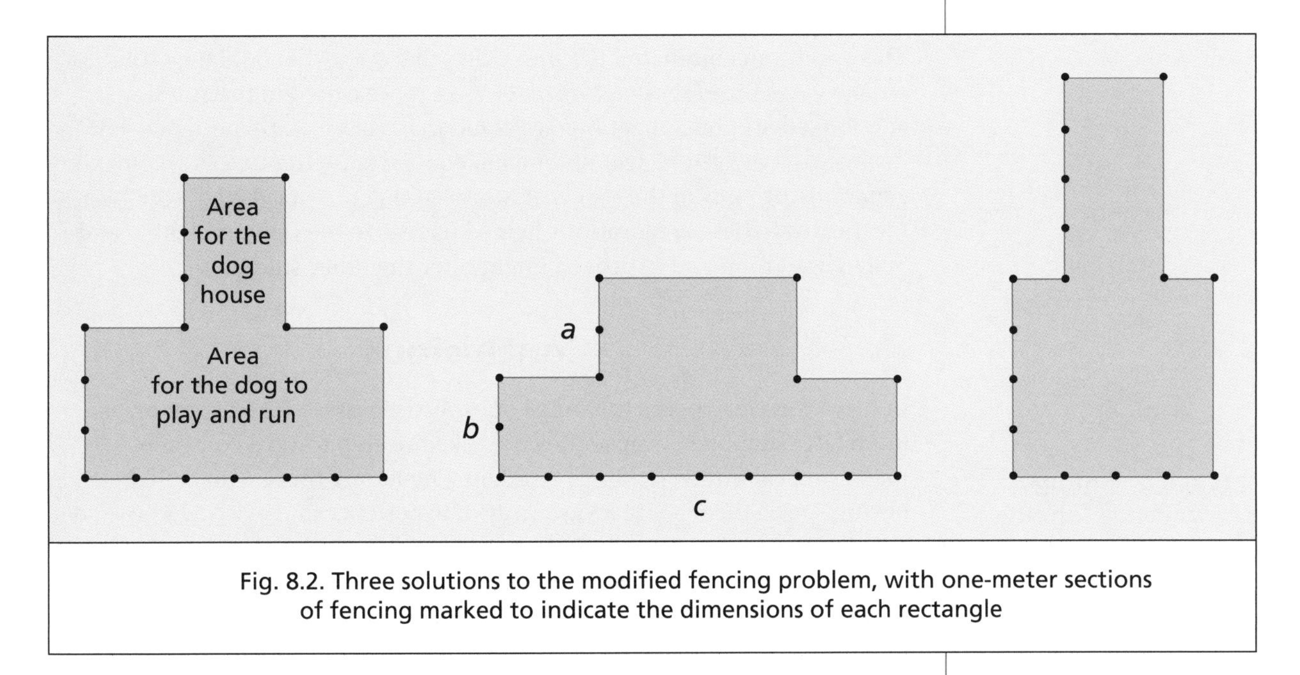

Fig. 8.2. Three solutions to the modified fencing problem, with one-meter sections of fencing marked to indicate the dimensions of each rectangle

Our exploration of the new problem unearthed significant mathematics and challenged our problem-solving skills. We began by creating a table of possibilities given that the sum of the areas of the two rectangles was 24. Our table included 23 + 1, 22 + 2, ..., 12 + 12. We then factored each area to find the possible dimensions of each rectangle. For example, 18 + 6 yielded 18×1, 9×2, 6×3, and 1×6, 2×3. We then made note that the perimeter of the dog pen could be found with the formula $P = 2a + 2b + 2c$, where a, b, and c were three of the four sides of the two rectangles as illustrated in figure 8.2. Only three sides were used to compute the perimeter, because twice the measure of side c accounted for the sum of the horizontal sides of the dog pen and the sum of twice the measures of sides a and b accounted for the sum of the vertical sides of the dog pen. For example, when we paired rectangles with dimensions 9×2 and 2×3, we found two possible perimeters by changing the orientation of the 2×3 rectangle: $2(2) + 2(2) + 2(9)$ and $2(3) + 2(2) + 2(9)$. The two pens formed from this pairing did not yield a perimeter of 24, but writing these expressions helped us notice that we could remove a common factor of 2 to get $12 = a + b + c$. We could then simplify our exploration to a search for pairs of rectangles for which the sum of $a + b + c$ was 12 [factor sum].

Using this method we quickly realized that our area sum 16 + 8 would yield more than one solution: 8×2 and 2×4, whose factor sum is 8 + 2 + 2 = 12; and 4×4 and 4×2, whose factor sum is 4 + 4 + 4 = 12. We also used our understandings of sums and products of even and odd numbers to eliminate possible solutions. Because 24 was the sum of two areas, we knew that both areas had to be either odd or even. If the addends were both odd, then all the factors had to be odd as well. For example, if we consider areas of 9 and 15, then the factors are all odd. We also knew that because the sum of three factors of the areas was half the perimeter, or 12, then either two addends were odd or all three addends were even. This condition eliminated the possibility that 9 and 15 could be a solution. Finally we realized that factors of 24 were represented in the solutions and looked for generalizations we could make from our experience. For instance, if we used 36 feet of fencing, could we use the factors to quickly generate dog pens of the sort that Stacey and Penny suggested were best for the dog? These explorations helped us realize the richness Penny and Stacey's solution and approach might offer the other students.

Conclusions

In inclusion classrooms the range of expertise possessed by students is often left untapped because they are asked to step toward common mathematical understandings. Students, including those who are labeled as having special needs, use a vast array of experience and existing knowledge as they attempt to answer problems they and their teachers pose. In these attempts they make assumptions that include interpretations of problem contexts and the mathematics involved, a process we refer to as self-differentiating. Considering students' alternative interpretations in such a way recasts the teacher's perspective from evaluation to inquisitiveness: how were you thinking about this problem, and what strategies did you use in reaching a solution? This approach to students' work has the potential to recognize the mathematical thinking of students rather than simply look for "errors."

Students, including those who are labeled as having special needs, use a vast array of experience and existing knowledge as they attempt to answer problems they and their teachers pose.

In inclusion classrooms in which exploration and problem solving are the bases for the discussions of mathematical ideas, teachers must take on very complex roles. Deciding how to pursue the mathematics involved in students' solutions involves making decisions quickly. Teachers necessarily make "judgments on the fly" using their analysis of students' solutions drawn from observations made during investigations of a problem. Our exploration of Stacey and Penny's solution serves as a cautionary tale regarding the expectation of approaches that might meet an initial objective. The girls' solution did, indeed, explore a crucial link between perimeter and area, albeit not in the ways the teacher expected. Although many teachers feel pressure to fulfill the mathematical objectives of a lesson, our work encourages them to explore the mathematics of the students (Steffe 1990). This disposition may allow the emergence of a trusting relationship between all students and their teacher that can support the mathematical, social, and emotional goals of each student.

REFERENCES

Cobb, Paul, Terri Wood, and Erna Yackel. "Classrooms as Learning Environments for Teachers and Researchers." In *Constructivist Views on the Teaching and Learning of Mathematics, Journal for Research in Mathematics Education* Monograph no. 4, edited by Robert B. Davis, Carolyn A. Maher, and Nel Noddings, pp. 125–46. Reston, Va.: National Council of Teachers of Mathematics, 1990.

Lappan, Glenda, James T. Fey, William M. Fitzgerald, Susan N. Friel, and Elizabeth D. Phillips. *Covering and Surrounding: Two-Dimensional Measurement.* Connected Mathematics Project: Geometry. Upper Saddle River, N.J.: Prentice Hall, 2002.

National Council of Teachers of Mathematics (NCTM). *Principles and Standards for School Mathematics.* Reston, Va.: NCTM, 2000.

Steffe, Leslie P. "On the Knowledge of Mathematics Teachers." In *Constructivist Views on the Teaching and Learning of Mathematics, Journal for Research in Mathematics Education* Monograph no. 4, edited by Robert B. Davis, Carolyn A. Maher, and Nel Noddings, pp. 167–84. Reston, Va.: National Council of Teachers of Mathematics, 1990.

von Glasersfeld, Ernst. *Radical Constructivism: A Way of Knowing and Seeing.* Washington, D.C.: Falmer Press, 1995.

Williams, Steven R., and Juliet A. Baxter. "Dilemmas of Discourse-Oriented Teaching in One Middle School Mathematics Classroom." *Elementary School Journal* 97 (September 1996): 21–38.

Woodward, John, and Marjorie Montague. "Meeting the Challenge of Mathematics Reform for Students with LD." *Journal of Special Education* 36 (Summer 2002): 89–101.

9

My Students Aren't Motivated—What Can I Do?

Matt Jones

"What difference does it make what I do?
My students aren't motivated."

As a mathematics education professional developer with hundreds of hours of experience working with teachers from second grade through college, I have often heard the refrain above. Lack of motivation is always a concern for teachers of mathematics, especially in the middle school years. Studies show that the middle school years are a crucial point in students' mathematical education during which much care must be taken to foster students' motivation. Ryan and Patrick (2001) refer to early adolescence as a "particularly precarious stage regarding changes in achievement beliefs and behavior" (p. 439). Thankfully, you as a teacher can do a great deal to increase students' motivation. In this article, I discuss techniques used by middle school teachers both classroomwide and with individual students, including students who often have difficulty understanding why they are learning mathematics. The teachers I have worked with agree that motivational strategies can help make "mathematics for every student" a reality.

The teachers I have worked with agree that motivational strategies can help make "mathematics for every student" a reality.

In this article I briefly explain motivational theory and then explore strategies that can be used to increase significant aspects of students' motivation. This explanation is followed by a discussion of additional techniques that can be used with students who need more individualized motivational support. Finally, I include a self-check questionnaire at the end of the article to help you measure your own progress as you implement these strategies. My presumption throughout this discussion is that all students have the potential to succeed in learning mathematics and that this outcome will be more likely to occur when they are motivated to do so.

What Is Motivation?

Several theories of motivation exist, and each emphasizes different elements as being important measures of motivation. *Expectancy-value* theory (Wigfield and Eccles 2000) is built around the notion that students are motivated when they expect that they can complete the task with reasonable effort and when they value the task, either for its own intrinsic enjoyment or for some other reason (for the learning gained from it, to please a parent or teacher, to avoid embarrassment, and so on). *Self-determination* theory sets motivation in a context of three basic human needs: relatedness, competence, and autonomy (Deci and Ryan 2000). In studying these theories and comparing them with findings specific to mathematics classrooms, such as those found in Middleton and Spanias's (1999) review of prior research, two core elements of instruction emerge as important to fostering students' motivation: (1) lesson design and implementation, and (2) learning environment. Here, the motivational aspects of each of these elements is described principally in terms of these theories and followed by examples and guidelines for teachers' actions that increase students' motivation.

Lesson Design and Implementation

Motivation is not inherent in the mathematics content. Instead, motivation lies within students and comes from their interaction with the content as embedded in a lesson's design and its implementation in the classroom. In this sense, motivation can be learned and developed (or diminished) on the basis of the ways in which you plan and implement your lessons. Thus, a lot of students' motivation can come from what they learn from you, the teacher (Brophy 2004; Middleton and Spanias 1999). I next describe three important characteristics of lesson design and implementation that help increase motivation in students: (1) contextualizing the mathematics, (2) exploring multiple solutions, and (3) providing task choice.

Contextualizing the Mathematics

What is contextualization? Contextualization, as it is used here, refers to a real-life context. Why is contextualization important for motivation? One of the major implications of motivation theory is that the age-old question "Why are we doing this?" has real legitimacy because it affects the value students place on the mathematics. If we want students to value the mathematics *in the classroom,* we need to be able to regularly point out how it is used *outside the classroom.* According to Middleton and Spanias (2002, p. 13),

> The best research available indicates that contextualization is beneficial in at least three ways: (*a*) It piques students' interest; (*b*) it stimulates students' imaginations and assists in drawing connections among mathematical and everyday concepts that children hold; and (*c*) it provides functional mathematical knowledge that is useful in a variety of applications.

As you look at the examples below, think about how students are more likely to value the mathematics they learn when they see its application in context, and how they are more likely to feel competent in making sense of the problem because of the presence of a context.

Integer Sums and Elevators

In learning about sums of integers, students may be asked to balance the books of a business, with payments (negative values) and revenue (positive values). As a second context, in the United States the ground floor is often labeled "G" and floors below it are "B1, B2, ..." or "P1, P2, ..." By connecting this experience with the practice in such countries as Scotland, where the ground floor is 0 and floors below it are numbered with negative integers (as in fig. 9.1), students also have the opportunity to make sense of the mathematics.

Fig. 9.1. Photo taken by author at Loch Ness Castle Urquhart tourist center

In a different area of mathematics, students learning about proportions may be asked, "If an 80-minute CD uses 70 megabytes of space on an iPod, how many minutes of music can be put on an iPod Shuffle, which holds 1000 megabytes (1 gigabyte) of music?"

Fractions in Real Life

You can also point out additional ways in which mathematical topics are used outside the classroom. For instance, why do we study fractions? Those who can do mental mathematics with fractions can compute the discounts for items on sale at the store. Some stock markets have prices that are set in increments of 1/32 of a dollar. Musicians have a working knowledge of addition of fractions, especially halves, quarters, and eighths, and have their own special ways of denoting such fractions as sixths or tenths (using triplets and quintuplets, respectively). Recipes use fractions of a cup, and those who want to make partial recipes have to multiply fractions. Fractions also represent fair sharing: five people sharing three sub sandwiches get three-fifths of a sandwich, two people sharing a dozen eggs each get one-half dozen, and so forth.

Interviews with Adults Who Use Mathematics

Having students talk with adults outside the school community about mathematics can also be an effective way to illustrate real-world uses of mathematics. One teacher I know has students interview someone they know and ask how they use mathematics at work. Each student then reports a summary of the interview for the class. Another teacher's extension of this idea is to have the student interview the speaker as a way of preparing the speaker to visit the class, then to invite the speaker to class to discuss the mathematics he or she uses at work.

Having students talk with adults outside the school community about mathematics can also be an effective way to illustrate real-world uses of mathematics.

From these examples, what can we learn about important considerations for contextualization? As the teacher, you are the authority on your students' interests (more on this later). Since different students have different interests, a useful tactic is to vary your choice of contexts. If your textbook does not offer a real-life context, or you do not think the context it provides is appropriate for your students, many resources for contextualized lessons can be found on the Web, including NCTM's Illuminations site (illuminations.nctm.org). When choosing a context, think carefully about how likely it is to activate students' existing knowledge (and thus their feelings of competence) and whether the context will be of interest to students (and to which students?).

Exploring Multiple Solutions

Reform in mathematics teaching often includes a call for exploring multiple solutions (NCTM 2000). From a perspective guided by research on motivation, several reasons can be cited for doing so. First, the opportunity to solve problems using methods selected by students gives them a degree of autonomy. Second, by legitimizing multiple solution methods, a greater proportion of students feel increased competence. Furthermore, exploring students' strategies, even those that lead to incorrect solutions, shows that you value the ideas they used and can lead to greater mathematical understanding for the entire class.

Students' Reasoning about Proportion

For example, here is a problem involving proportions: A student, Tara, can walk the length of the classroom, 30 feet, in 15 steps. Her teacher can walk the same 30 feet in just 12 steps. How many more steps will Tara need to take, compared with her teacher, to walk the school hallway, which is 180 feet long? Students who solve this problem correctly may work multiplicatively, seeing that because $6 \times 30 = 180$, Tara will take 6×15, or 90, steps, and her teacher will take 6×12, or 72, steps. Others will repeatedly add 15 steps and 30 feet, and 12 steps and 30 feet, until they cover the 180-foot length of the hallway. One common misconception is to think of this problem in an additive way, reasoning that if Tara takes 3 more steps than her teacher over 30 feet, then Tara will also take 3 steps more when walking the 180-foot hallway. As discussed further in the next section, in a learning community, if a student volunteers this erroneous answer, rather than immediately correct the student, the teacher would invite the student to share his or her reasoning, and then either the teacher or fellow students would work to dissuade the student with alternative reasoning. In response to the error in proportional reasoning mentioned above, one teacher decided that the best way to convince his students was to actually pace the length of the classroom himself and then to have a (much shorter) student do the same. The teacher and student then paced the length of the hallway with the class helping to keep count of their steps. Through this demonstration, the student who used additive reasoning and those who had agreed with it could directly confront their misconception and have it dispelled.

In a learning community, if a student volunteers this erroneous answer, rather than immediately correct the student, the teacher would invite the student to share his or her reasoning, and then either the teacher or fellow students would work to dissuade the student with alternative reasoning.

In the foregoing example, we see how students can have the autonomy to choose a method that makes sense to them, and how their misconceptions can be challenged in a way that respects their thinking and makes them feel they are competent at mathematics, even if they are not always correct. An exploration of multiple solutions begins with problems that invite multiple approaches. Contextual problems often work for this purpose: students' existing knowledge of the context helps them think of ways to attack the problem. When students are sharing solutions, the teacher should withhold immediate judgment of the correctness of a solution, and instead invite students to support or disagree with the answer through mathematical reasoning. When students are discussing their reasoning, the teacher should remind students that (1) they may criticize ideas, not other students; and (2) wrong answers help everyone understand the problem better and decrease the likelihood of students' making those mistakes later.

Providing Task Choice

Providing task choice is a simple way to promote students' sense of autonomy in the classroom. Deci and Ryan (2000) reviewed multiple studies and concluded that supporting autonomy through choice was associated with positive outcomes, such as greater intrinsic motivation, increased satisfaction, and enhanced well-being. In addition, students will often choose the tasks they find most interesting, thereby increasing the value aspect of their motivation. I next describe ways to provide task choice and then highlight the most important considerations when determining what choices to give to students.

Two common places to provide choice are on homework and on longer-term projects. On homework, the differences between problems may focus on applying the same mathematics in different contexts. On longer projects, teachers can offer choice by giving several possible projects for students to choose from. Alternatively, if projects are regularly assigned throughout the school year, you might tell students that they may opt to skip a select number (perhaps one or two).

The principal guideline in providing task choice is that students should feel that the choices differ significantly enough so that their selections are meaningful. For example, students who get to choose to do either the even-numbered exercises or the odd-numbered exercises are not likely to think that a meaningful difference exists between them, since the difficulty level and number of problems are likely to be similar. However, students who get to choose between a problem that is set in the context of bicycling and a problem involving music would be likely to perceive this choice as meaningful.

Learning Environment

The suggestions about lesson design and implementation could perhaps be described as ways to connect students with the content to increase their motivation. Another important principle of motivation theory is that the classroom norms and climate that you establish have a significant effect on students' motivation. This section focuses on the personal side of the classroom—the connections made between you and your students—and the learning atmosphere you create. The development of a classroom that students perceive as having a positive, supportive climate is a strong predictor of students' motivation (Stipek et al. 1998). If you can establish your classroom as a learning community, a place in which everyone is gathered to learn from one another, you will increase students' intrinsic motivation to succeed. I next discuss three significant actions needed to build a learning community: (1) connecting with your students on a personal level; (2) establishing cooperation in the classroom; and (3) emphasizing the role and importance of effort and learning.

Connecting with Your Students

The connection between you and your students is vital to their motivation. The rapport you build with your students helps meet their need for relatedness. Teachers who develop healthy relationships with their students, in which students know that they are valued and cared about as people, give students confidence and feelings of self-worth (Covington 1984). You are better equipped to connect with your students if you make an effort to know about their interests and their lives. Although any time can be a good time to get to know your students, the beginning of the year represents an opportunity to have all students respond in writing to a few questions about themselves, such as, "What do you like to do when you're not in school?" "Do you have any hobbies?" or "What is your favorite TV show or video game?" With the information you gather, you are better able to choose problem contexts likely to interest your students. In addition, you have an opportunity to learn a bit about students' home life, perhaps by asking, "Who lives with you?" and "What language(s) are spoken in your home?" Another tactic practiced by many teachers is to greet each student individually as she or he enters the classroom. Finally, you can also share an occasional story about yourself (perhaps detailing a situation in which you used mathematics outside of teaching!). The guiding premise for all these actions is that you want to show students that teachers are people and that you care about your students as people, not just as learners of mathematics.

Establishing Cooperation in the Classroom

A second important connection for students is their interaction with peers. This connection is central to meeting students' needs for relatedness. Students in cooperative classrooms (defined below) report an increased sense of efficacy, increased value, and a greater orientation toward mastering the content (Miller and Hertz-Lazarowitz 1992; Nichols and Miller 1994; Slavin 1995, 1996).

The guiding norm for a cooperative learning community is "*We're all in this together, learning and helping one another learn*" (Brophy 2004, p. 202, emphasis in original). When teaching students to work cooperatively, the ultimate goal is to have them learn how to respect one another as people, and also to listen and attend to one another's ideas. Effective cooperative learning environments happen when the teacher helps students learn the skills necessary to work collaboratively in small groups. Students need to be clear about how to treat fellow group members with respect, how to make sure everyone contributes, and how to provide assistance to one another in a way that focuses not on the answer but on helping one's fellow group members learn (Johnson and Johnson 1999; Slavin 1995, 1996). Such skills can be taught through role-play in which the teacher and a student volunteer explicitly model acceptable behavior as well as inappropriate actions. Once interpersonal skills have been taught, students are likely to need regular reminders about how to fulfill their roles within their groups and the classroom. Some teachers post reminders about student roles on the walls of their rooms, and refer students to them whenever a group assignment is given.

Emphasizing the Role and Importance of Effort and Learning

One of the most important factors in establishing a learning community is for the teacher to guide students to understand the meaning of success. In a mathematics learning community, success means working hard to understand mathematics (Middleton and Spanias 2002) and progressing toward personal learning goals. To foster these notions, the teacher must communicate through words and actions that everyone is expected to give his or her best effort to learning mathematics.

Students often come to mathematics class with the misconception that people succeed in mathematics primarily because of natural ability and that those who have to work hard are just not "math smart." This belief becomes more pervasive as students progress through school (see NAEP survey data reported by Mitchell et al. [1999]). To counteract this belief, you should explicitly discuss the importance of effort in determining success in your class. You should also avoid comparing students' abilities. Instead, recognize students' improvement over the year with oral or written comments to individuals. In addition, you can encourage students to measure and notice their own progress by keeping a portfolio of their work and requiring them to write journal reflections discussing how the quality of their work has improved and how the amount of mathematics they understand has increased. You can also encourage students to evaluate the quality of their work by giving them a rubric and asking them to apply it to their own project or portfolio. Giving students an active role in their own learning is one way to foster their sense of autonomy in the class. Finally, you can show that you value improvement and effort by allowing students to retake or revise poor work. In this way, you show students that what matters is not whether they "get it" on the first try but whether they persist until they have learned the material.

Giving students an active role in their own learning is one way to foster their sense of autonomy in the class.

This definition of success also means helping students attribute the source of difficulties or failures appropriately. Students who are more successful in learning mathematics typically attribute their failures to the use of an inappropriate solution strategy or to a lack of effort, both of which are controllable causes (Middleton and Spanias 1999). As with the "multiple solutions" example, students should be helped to explore the reasons for their mistakes and therefore to gain from them not only a better understanding of the mathematics but also the insight that the source of their difficulty was not an internal, uncontrollable cause, such as lack of ability. These practices help students develop their sense of competence in mathematics. The principle to keep in mind is that students come to believe in effort when your policies and actions, along with your words, emphasize that effort matters.

Strategies for Individuals in Need of Extra Motivational Support

If you have worked to develop lesson tasks that are contextual with multiple pathways to a solution, have permitted students autonomy in choosing some assignments, and have established a cooperative learning community in your classroom, you are well on your way to improving students' motivation to learn mathematics. However, not all students will respond to these general strategies. Although research emphasizes that extrinsic rewards should be minimized in educational contexts because they can erode intrinsic motivation, some students need more than what general, classroomwide tactics can achieve. Brophy (1996 2004) suggests that students who display few interests and little motivation may be candidates for the strategic use of extrinsic rewards. In doing so, the teacher should consider a few important guidelines on structuring rewards. Rewards should not be so valuable or ostentatious that they are a complete distraction from the real goal, which is students' learning. They should, if possible, be naturally related to the behavior. Finally, they should be contingent on achieving specific goals.

In some instances, a contract may be set up with specific provisions for how the student may earn rewards. An advisable approach in setting up a contract is to enter into it cooperatively with your student rather than impose a contract without the student's input. In this way, the student gains some autonomy in setting the conditions and rewards, and can feel some ownership in helping to improve himself or herself. For example, a student who has not been completing his or her homework might arrange with you to earn a sticker for every two homework assignments that he or she completes. After earning several stickers, the student might win a pencil or other small reward. The student should not win a reward that undermines the premise that learning mathematics is the primary goal, such as a homework pass. Remember, if you establish yourself as a caring person and show respect for the student and her or his needs, you are laying the groundwork for a cooperative relationship in which the student breaks bad habits and increases her or his learning.

Conclusion

"Mathematics for every student" can become a reality in your classroom. But for this outcome to occur, teachers need to develop in students the motivation to realize their fullest potential. You have seen in this article that motivation is not a singular attribute, but instead that different aspects of each student's motivation are affected both by the lessons they experience and the environment in which they learn. Therefore, you maximize the likelihood of fostering students' motivation by building lessons that promote students' feelings of autonomy and competence and their belief in the value of mathematics while also working toward establishing a learning environment that supports students' needs for relatedness and cooperation. To help you monitor your success in targeting the four main aspects of motivation discussed in this article (value, competence or expectancy, autonomy, relatedness), I have provided the self-monitoring checklist in figure 9.2.

Teacher Action	Consistently	Not Often Enough
Tasks and Assignments		
Do I provide tasks that encourage students to see the *value* of the mathematics being learned by using contextual problems?		
Do I provide students the *autonomy* to choose their roles in group tasks?		
Do I provide students *autonomy* on out-of-class assignments, such as homework and projects?		
Do I foster students' sense of *competence* by providing problems of appropriate difficulty?		
Do I foster students' sense of *competence* by encouraging them to use, explain, and defend their own methods for solving those problems?		
Classroom Learning Environment		
Do I meet students' need for *relatedness* by trying to get to know them and their interests, and using that information in my lessons?		
Do I meet students' need for *relatedness* by encouraging them and teaching them how to collaborate to help one another learn rather than compete with one another?		
Do I foster students' feelings of *competence* by encouraging them to evaluate their own learning?		
Do I foster students' feelings of *competence* by recognizing improvement in individual students?		
Do I foster students' feelings of *competence* by giving them opportunities to improve their work?		

Fig. 9.2. Motivation self-monitoring checklist for teachers

By teaching students the value of mathematics, helping them realize that they possess the ability to be successful in mathematics, and providing a supportive learning environment, teachers help most students begin to realize that doing well in mathematics is both in their best interest and within their ability. For those who are slower to come around, developing a cooperative relationship and establishing specific goal-setting routines will achieve steady improvement. Motivation is essential to achieving mathematics for all. Take advantage of the strategies research has found effective in building students' motivation to learn.

REFERENCES

Brophy, Jere. *Teaching Problem Students.* New York: Guilford Press, 1996.

———. *Motivating Students to Learn.* Mahwah, N.J.: Lawrence Erlbaum Associates, 2004.

Covington, Martin V. "The Self-Worth Theory of Achievement Motivation: Findings and Implications." *Elementary School Journal* 85 (1984): 5–20.

Deci, Edward L., and Richard M. Ryan. "The 'What' and 'Why' of Goal Pursuits: Human Needs and the Self-Determination of Behavior." *Psychological Inquiry* 11 (2000): 227–68.

Johnson, David W., and Roger T. Johnson. *Learning Together and Alone: Cooperative, Competitive, and Individualistic Learning.* 5th ed. Boston: Allyn & Bacon, 1999.

Middleton, James A., and Photini A. Spanias." Motivation for Achievement in Mathematics: Findings, Generalizations, and Criticisms of the Research." *Journal for Research in Mathematics Education* 30 (1999): 65–88.

———. "Findings from Research on Motivation in Mathematics Education: What Matters in Coming to Value Mathematics." In *Lessons Learned from Research,* edited by Judith Sowder and Bonnie Schappelle, pp. 9–15. Reston, Va.: NCTM, 2002.

Miller, Norman, and Rachel Hertz-Lazarowitzeds. *Interaction in Cooperative Groups: The Theoretical Anatomy of Group Learning.* New York: Cambridge University Press, 1992.

Mitchell, Julia H., Evelyn F. Hawkins, Pamela M. Jakwerth, Frances B. Stancavage, and John A. Dossey. *Student Work and Teacher Practices in Mathematics.* Washington, D.C.: National Center for Education Statistics, 1999.

National Council of Teachers of Mathematics (NCTM). *Principles and Standards for School Mathematics.* Reston, Va.: NCTM, 2000.

Nichols, Joe D., and Raymond B. Miller. "Cooperative Learning and Student Motivation." *Contemporary Educational Psychology* 19 (1994): 167–78.

Ryan, Allison M., and Helen Patrick. "The Classroom Social Environment and Changes in Adolescents' Motivation and Engagement during Middle School." *American Educational Research Journal* 38 (2001): 437–60.

Slavin, Robert E. *Cooperative Learning: Theory, Research, and Practice.* 2nd ed. Boston: Allyn & Bacon, 1995.

———. "Research on Cooperative Learning and Achievement: What We Know, What We Need to Know." *Contemporary Educational Psychology* 21 (1996): 43–69.

Stipek, Deborah, Julie M. Salmon, Karen B. Givvin, Elham Kazemi, Geoffrey Saxe, and Valanne L. Macgyvers. "The Value (and Convergence) of Practices Suggested by Motivation Research and Promoted by Mathematics Education Reformers." *Journal for Research in Mathematics Education* 29 (July 1998): 465–88.

Wigfield, Alan L., and Jacqueline S. Eccles. "Expectancy-Value Theory of Achievement Motivation." *Contemporary Educational Psychology* 25 (2000): 68–81.

10

Approaches to Assessing Students' Thinking from Analyzing Errors in Homework

Shuhua An
Zhonghe Wu

Errors are a positive thing in the process of learning—or at least they should be. In many cultures, errors are regarded as an opportunity to reflect and learn.

—*Robert B. Ashlock*

HOMEWORK can be a powerful tool for learning and teaching when teachers carefully analyze it for insights into how students are making sense of mathematics (An 2004). Such an approach provides a lens for the teacher in diagnosing learner problems, through which the teacher views students' thinking at a deep, internal level and provides timely feedback to clarify misconceptions. Furthermore, through analyzing students' error patterns from homework, the teacher is able to gain insight into their misconceptions, to adjust instruction according to students' needs, and to develop students' mathematical understanding (An 2000, 2004). Realizing that the time teachers have available to review homework is limited, in this article we describe the use of a systematic sampling method for analyzing homework.

The Importance of Analyzing Errors in Homework

The importance of assessing students' thinking from analyzing homework is made clear in our model of how students' knowledge develops and the stages at which a teacher can assess students' proficiency and provide timely feedback (fig.10.1). Early in the learning sequence, a teacher assesses students' thinking from observation, questions, and interviews while teaching in the classroom. The teacher is able to identify some of the students' misconceptions and can provide feedback immediately at this stage. However, the teacher knows only part of the students' thinking—their reflexive thinking about the knowledge just learned, which has not been fully internalized.

Note: This article discusses data collected as a part of a study supported by an AERA-OERI grant in 2003.

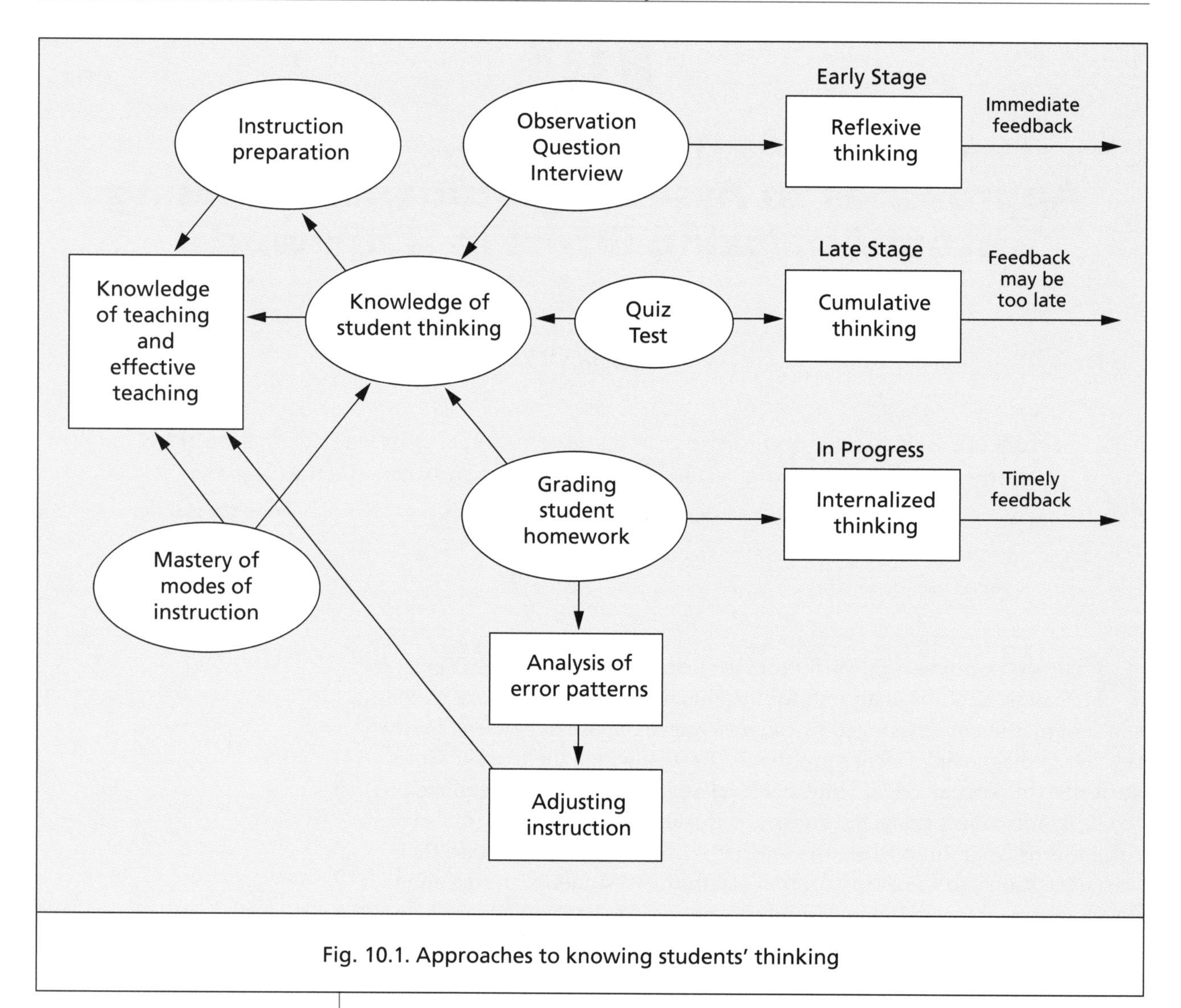

Fig. 10.1. Approaches to knowing students' thinking

It is crucial that a teacher assesses students' thinking from analyzing homework, because homework often involves knowledge that is "in process" or being internalized and, as such, is still open to revision.

Later, a teacher assesses students' thinking through formal assessment, such as a quiz or a test. However, since a quiz or a test assesses students' knowledge that has developed over a longer period of time, students' misconceptions might have existed for quite a while. The teacher's feedback at this stage may be too little, too late to correct error patterns that have become ingrained.

It is crucial that a teacher assesses students' thinking from analyzing homework, because homework often involves knowledge that is "in process" or being internalized and, as such, is still open to revision. To do homework, students need not only to recall, review, and understand the concepts and skills learned from the classroom but also to apply them to solve problems independently. The process of recalling, reviewing, understanding, and applying is a process of internalizing knowledge and skills learned in classwork. This internalization enables students to transfer and construct knowledge learned from others, making it their own (An 2004). When looking over students' homework papers, the teacher can notice error patterns and clarify students' misconceptions before they become fully internalized and more resistant to change. Such analysis can also help teachers identify diverse students' learning needs, assess their different levels of understanding, and design various strategies to support student learning in a variety of ways.

In the study, homework is defined as a task that gives students an opportunity to practice and reinforce their learned knowledge and skills to be ready for new lessons; grading homework refers to a teacher's evaluating students' understanding in their independent practice and analyzing patterns of misconceptions.

The Process of Analyzing Errors from Homework

The authors conducted a homework study, based on the conceptual framework in figure 10.1, with five classroom teachers of fifth to eighth grade in Los Angeles County in 2003. We focused on what teachers learned about students' thinking from grading homework, analyzing error patterns, correcting misconceptions, and adjusting their lessons according to the evidence of students' proficiency as indicated by their homework. The teachers in this study had five periods of 30–40 students per class and had indicated to us that they do not have time to thoroughly examine and evaluate each student's homework daily. Before engaging in this study, most of the teachers in the study graded homework on effort and completion. For example, Mr. Nelson, a sixth-grade teacher in this study, described his way of grading homework: "I grade it in terms of completion and effort.... Homework is graded in class. Students correct their own papers.... We often spend up to 30 minutes on homework." Ms. Sedillos, another teacher in this study, agreed: "I do not grade each problem. I grade solely on completion...." Considering that U.S. teachers usually do not have sufficient time to grade all students' homework daily, the teachers in this study were trained in using a four-step sampling method for grading students' homework and analyzing students' error patterns, as described below:

1. Analyze students' state test scores from previous year and district pretests to assign students to one of three groups: "proficient," "somewhat proficient," and "not yet proficient." Make necessary changes to these groups on the basis of each student's performance during the school year.
2. Collect and grade a sample of students' homework from each group by selecting six to nine students each day, consisting of two to three from each group, to have a wide range of representation from different levels of proficiency.
3. Write a brief grading log each day, and analyze errors:
   - Original records of errors (copy complete problem and students' work)
   - Analysis of types of errors: conceptual, procedural, and careless errors

- Analysis of the cause of errors
- Approaches to making correction of misconceptions

4. Use the results of homework analysis to correct misconceptions:
    - Whole-class instruction if the errors appear in at least two groups and the errors are main conceptual and procedural errors
    - Individualized correction if the errors occur only in the "not yet proficient" group
    - Other methods of correction, such as group correction if the "proficient" group makes no error, so they can help others in the group correction or self-correction if most errors are careless errors

The teachers also learned a technique for selecting "sample" students using the grading-record chart and daily grading log, which are described in the sections that follow.

Figure 10.2 shows a sample of a grading-record chart from fifth-grade teacher Ms. Sedillos. The first column with names of students is deleted. Column 2 shows the scores of students on their previous unit's exam (or beginning-of-the-year pretest), from the lowest score, 53, to highest score, 97. These scores served as the basis for classifying students into three levels of proficiency. Students were regrouped at the end of each unit on the basis of their demonstrated achievement. From column 3 to the rightmost edge, lessons in each week are indicated. Each day, the teacher selected eight students from three groups: two each from the "proficient" and "not yet proficient" groups (see the shaded areas) and four from the "somewhat proficient" group (see unshaded area).

For example, for lesson L3 in week 1, Ms. Sedillos graded the homework papers of eight students—two from the "proficient" group, four from the "somewhat proficient" group, and two from the "not yet proficient" group. For each homework assignment, Ms. Sedillos selected students whose work would graded, and each student had an equal chance to be selected during the unit. This selection process is important because it allows Ms. Sedillos to examine papers from every range of prior achievement and helps her know students' thinking at different proficiency levels.

After randomly selecting two to four students from each of the three groups, teachers graded each problem from their homework papers, analyzed the errors, developed a method for correcting misconceptions, adjusted lessons according to students' understanding as indicated from their homework, and kept grading logs in which they recorded and reflected on students' thinking.

After randomly selecting two to four students from each of the three groups, teachers graded each problem from their homework papers, analyzed the errors, developed a method for correcting misconceptions, adjusted lessons according to students' understanding as indicated from their homework, and kept grading logs in which they recorded and reflected on students' thinking. Figure 10.3 shows a grading-log entry for a lesson on fraction, decimal, and percent from sixth-grade teacher Mr. Nelson.

On a daily basis (presuming homework is assigned daily), every teacher in the study used the grading-log sheet to record students' errors, analyze the reasons for the errors, decide on ways of correcting errors, and indicate whether she or he would clarify the misconceptions through instruction, activity, or assessment. Detailed examples of these approaches are shared subsequently.

		Lessons in Week 1					**Lessons in Week 2**					**Lessons in Week 3**					
Name	**Score**	**L1**	**L2**	**L3**	**L4**	**L5**	**L1**	**L2**	**L3**	**L4**	**L5**	**L1**	**L2**	**L3**	**L4**	**L5**	**Group**
	53	X				X				X				X			
	57	X				X				X				X			
	58		X				X				X				X		
	60		X				X				X				X		Not yet proficient
	63			X				X				X				X	
	64			X				X				X				X	
	66				X				X				X				
	69				X				X				X				
	71				X				X				X				
	72				X				X				X				
	75			X				X				X				X	
	76			X				X				X				X	
	78		X				X				X				X		
	80		X				X				X				X		
	80	X				X				X				X			
	83	X				X				X				X			Somewhat proficient
	84	X				X				X				X			
	85	X				X				X				X			
	85		X				X				X				X		
	86		X				X				X				X		
	87			X				X				X				X	
	88			X				X				X				X	
	88				X				X				X				
	89				X				X				X				
	90				X				X				X				
	90				X				X				X				
	93			X				X				X				X	
	94			X				X				X				X	
	94		X				X				X				X		Proficient
	96		X				X				X				X		
	97	X				X				X				X			
	97	X				X				X				X			

Fig. 10.2. Sample of grading-record chart

Date: 4-11 Instructor: Nelson School: Spring Grade: 6 Topic: Percent, Fraction, Decimal								
Student	Errors	Reasons	Correcting Errors			Action of Correcting Error		
			Individual	Whole class	Other	Instruction	Activity	Assessment
#34 Not yet proficient	Wrote the decimal as a percent: 0.07 = 0.07%	Did not convert the decimal to a percent. Just placed a percent sign on the decimal. Lack of understanding of decimal place values and the meaning of percent.		X		X		X

Fig. 10.3. Sample of homework grading log

Examples of Error Analysis

The following are examples of two teachers' analyses of errors from homework during a unit on fraction, decimal, and percent. The teachers analyzed students' misconceptions on the basis of three types of errors: conceptual, procedural, and careless. These examples show that teachers are also learners who inquire about students' thinking, recognize patterns of errors, and take action to correct misconceptions and use errors to reinforce understanding. The teachers' active engagement in the process of error analysis provided evidence of their growth in gaining insight into students' thinking.

Ms. Sedillos's Error Analysis

Example 1: Ordering decimals

Ms. Sedillos, a fifth-grade teacher with five years of teaching experience, did the following error analysis (fig. 10.4) using homework from a lesson on ordering decimals. The examples show that Ms. Sedillos' knowledge of students' thinking has been enhanced as more analysis work has been done.

Problem	Error Pattern	Reasons	Correction	Action
Order each set of numbers from least to greatest: 8, 0.89, 0.38	8, 0.38, 0.89 Conceptual error	Read numbers as if there were no decimals	Correct this misconception individually	Address it through instruction—Place-value chart

Fig.10.4. Error analysis of ordering decimals

Ms. Sedillos identified the following misconception about decimals from the work of a student in the "not yet proficient" group: The student read numbers as if they had no decimal point, which implies the student ordered them as whole numbers (see fig. 10.4). Because of this misconception, some students think that the more digits a number has to the right of the decimal point, the greater its value. Conceptually, comparing decimal numbers is recognized as "require[ing] extending and generalizing the notion of whole number place value" (Sowder 1988, p. 188). However, children often do not easily understand this conceptual difference. In a study of sixth- and seventh-grade students' work, Hiebert and Wearne (1986) found that about half of the students believed that having more digits indicates a larger value. This misconception suggests that teachers must design instruction that helps students transition from whole numbers to decimals, explicitly helping students understand the similarities and differences between whole numbers and decimals. Realizing the importance of understanding decimals, Ms. Sedillos corrected this error individually on the student's paper and also face-to-face using a hundredths grid with all students in the "not yet proficient" group. In addition, to make sure all students understood comparing decimals conceptually, she addressed it in whole-class instruction using a place-value chart (see fig.10.5).

Ones	Tenths	Hundredths
8		
0	3	8
0	8	9

Fig. 10.5. Place-value chart

Ms. Sedillos directed students to compare the place values from left to right in the place-value chart. In the ones place, 0 is less than 8, so students knew 8 was the largest number. After that, students compared two numbers, 3 and 8, both at the tenths place. Since 3 is less than 8, students identified 38 < 89, which means .38 < .89. A study by Sowder and Markovits (1989) showed that using place-value units when comparing decimals helps students master the skill of ordering decimals.

An extension of the place-value chart involves representing the numbers visually with a grid model (Bennett and Nelson 2004). The grid squares can represent thousandths, hundredths, or tenths. For example, to compare 8, 0.38, and 0.89, teachers can use hundredths grids to help students see that although 0.38 has two digits, it has the smallest area; however, with just a single digit, 8 has the largest area (see fig. 10.6).

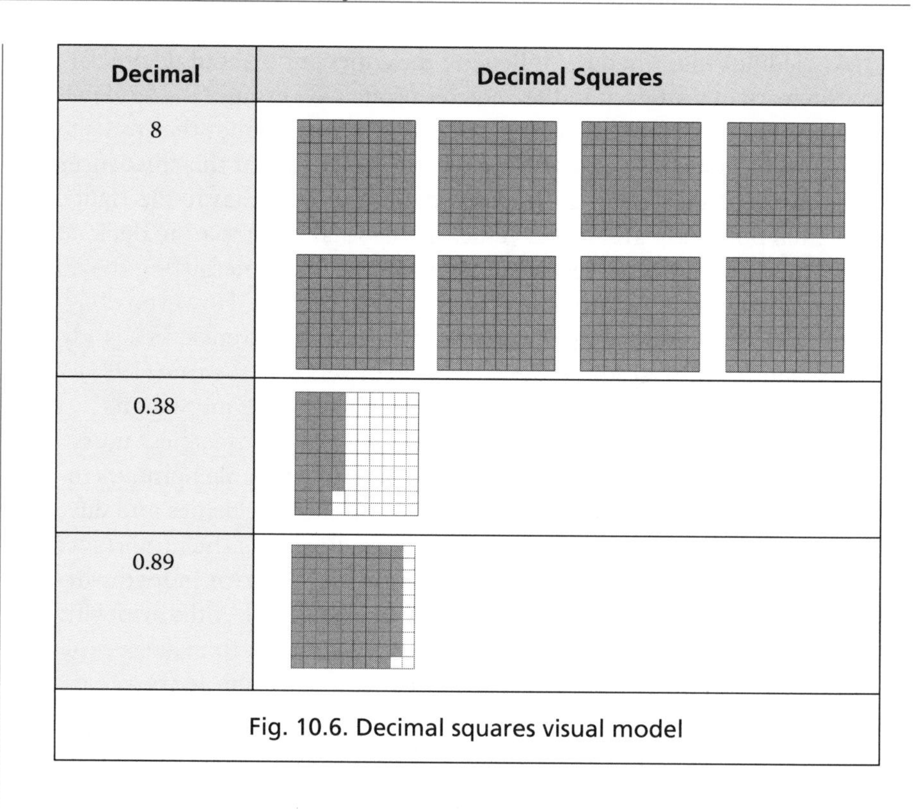

Decimal	Decimal Squares
8	
0.38	
0.89	

Fig. 10.6. Decimal squares visual model

Example 2: Equivalent fractions

Another lesson for which Ms. Sedillos analyzed students' homework focused on equivalent fractions. Figure 10.7 shows one error she found during this process.

Problem	Error Pattern	Reasons	Correction	Action
Find the missing number to make the fractions equivalent: $\frac{3}{5} = \frac{}{20}$	$\frac{3}{5} = \frac{4}{20}$ Conceptual error	Student put the number used to multiply the numerator to get the equivalent fraction as the numerator of the second fraction.	Correct this misconception with the whole class	Address it in instruction and activity—Fraction Tracks

Fig. 10.7. Error analysis of equivalent fractions

Ms. Sedillos realized that the student simply put 4 as the answer because that is the factor multiplied by 5 to make 20. She identified the misconception as being with the student's understanding of the concept of equivalence. When multiplying 4 by 5, one should also multiply 4 by 3 at the same time so as to have equivalent fractions:

$$\frac{3}{5} = \frac{3 \times 4}{5 \times 4} = \frac{12}{20}.$$

To correct this misconception and help students understand how to create equivalent fractions, Ms. Sedillos decided to bring it up with the whole class and to integrate this concept into instruction and assessment because "concepts such as the equivalence of rational numbers develop very slowly over time" (Ashlock 2006, p. 146). In her instruction, Mrs. Sedillos had students play the game Fraction Tracks, in which students use equivalent fractions in a race to be the first one to form a whole using number lines divided into various fractional lengths (Cathcart et al. 2001).

Mr. Nelson's Error Analysis

Mr. Nelson is a sixth-grade teacher with four years of teaching experience. His error analyses focused on students' difficulties with the division of fractions and the application of the distributive property when multiplying decimals.

Example 1: Division of fractions

Problem	Error Pattern	Reasons	Correction	Action
Divide: $3\frac{4}{5} \div 4$	$3\frac{4}{5} \div 4 = \frac{19}{5} \div 4 = \frac{5}{19} \times 4 = \frac{20}{19}$ Procedural error	Took the reciprocal of the dividend instead of the divisor	Correct this misconception with the whole class	Address it in activity and assessment

Fig. 10.8. Error analysis of dividing fractions

Mr. Nelson identified the error as taking the reciprocal of the dividend instead of the divisor. However, he did not realize that one difficulty in learning fraction division with this type of problem may be that 4 is not a fraction. Some students do not know that 4 can be written as 4/1, or have a misconception that a whole number cannot be written in fraction notation. According to the rule students likely memorized for fraction division, they need to multiply by a reciprocal. Since, in some students' view, the only available fraction is 19/5, they change it to 5/19. Often accompanying this sort of error is a student's lack of understanding of the concept of division. With such understanding, a student would clearly know that making four equal groups from

$$3\frac{4}{5}$$

would give less than 1 in each group. To clarify these misconceptions, the teacher might cultivate students' number sense in learning fractions. Mr. Nelson addressed the error with the whole class by writing down the three steps of mixed-number division: (1) changing the mixed number to an improper fraction, (2) changing the division sign to multiplication, and (3) taking the reciprocal of the divisor (second fraction). This approach, however, may not have been as effective as going back to reteach concepts of division and fraction.

An alternative approach to addressing the errors with the foregoing fraction division problem is offered by Huinker (2002), who has found that an important dimension of operation sense is to use properties of operations, such as distribution. Thus the teacher can help students solve this problem in the following way:

$$3\frac{4}{5} \div 4 = \left(3 + \frac{4}{5}\right) \div 4 = (3 \div 4) + \left(\frac{4}{5} \div 4\right) = \frac{3}{4} + \frac{4}{5} \times \frac{1}{4} = \frac{3}{4} + \frac{1}{5} = \frac{19}{20}.$$

To understand this type of problem conceptually and visually, the teacher can use visual representations and models to demonstrate the process of fraction division (An and Wu 2009). The process is based on the idea of taking some quantity and separating it into *n* equal parts, where *n* is the divisor. The following is an example of using a rectangular model for the problem

$$3\frac{4}{5} \div 4.$$

1. First represent the dividend

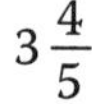

$$3\frac{4}{5}$$

by drawing four whole rectangles with five equal parts in each. The last one has only four parts out of the five shaded to show it is less than a whole. See figure 10.9.

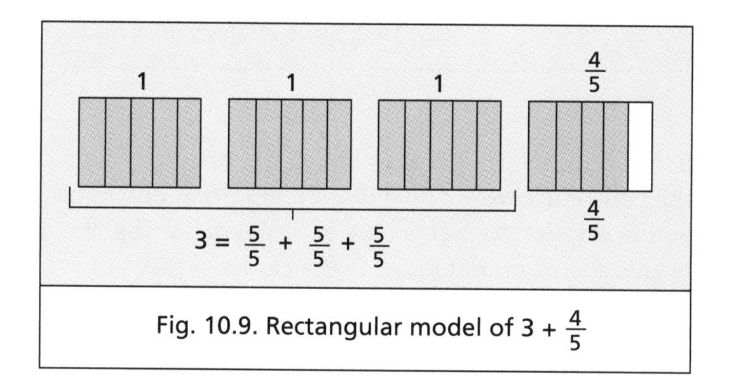

Fig. 10.9. Rectangular model of $3 + \frac{4}{5}$

2. Next, since the divisor is 4, divide each rectangle into four equal parts. See figure 10.10.

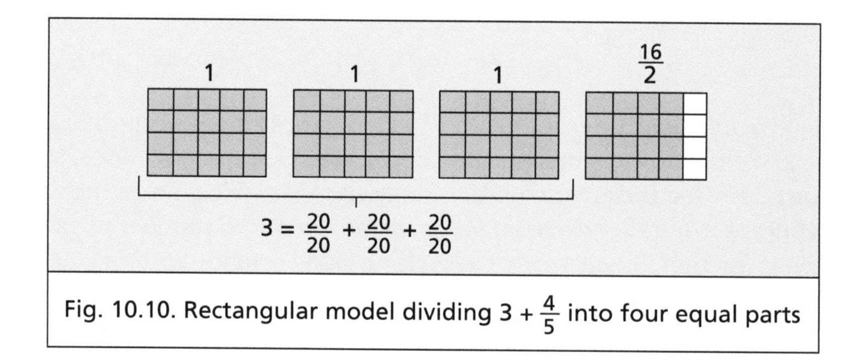

Fig. 10.10. Rectangular model dividing $3 + \frac{4}{5}$ into four equal parts

3. Finally, take 1/4 of each rectangle to represent the process of division by 4. See figure 10.11.

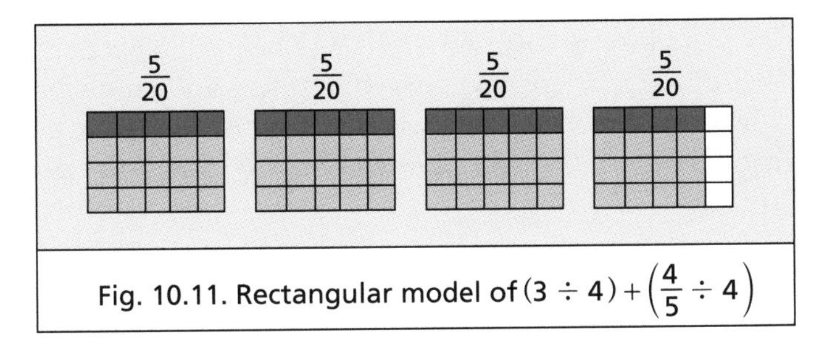

Fig. 10.11. Rectangular model of $(3 \div 4) + \left(\frac{4}{5} \div 4\right)$

So from figures 10.10 and 10.11, we have

$$3\frac{4}{5} \div 4 = \left(3 + \frac{4}{5}\right) \div 4 = (3 \div 4) + \left(\frac{4}{5} \div 4\right)$$

$$= \left[\left(\frac{5}{5} + \frac{5}{5} + \frac{5}{5}\right) \div 4\right] + \left(\frac{4}{5} \div 4\right) = \frac{5}{20} + \frac{5}{20} + \frac{5}{20} + \frac{4}{20} = \frac{19}{20}.$$

Example 2. Using distributive property with multiplication of decimals

Problem	Error Pattern	Reasons	Correction	Action
Complete the calculation using the distributive property and mental math: 12 (5.04) =12(5 + 0.04) = ?	12(5 + 0.04) = 60 + 48 = 1.08 Procedural error	He had trouble multiplying decimals: ex. 12(.04) = 48. He then tried to "move" the decimal in the sum.	Correct this misconception individually	Address it in activity and assessment

Fig.10.12. Error analysis of distributive property

Mr. Nelson knew that the student had trouble multiplying 12(0.04) and that the error, at a procedural level, involved moving the decimal before the multiplication (making 0.04 into 4) without understanding its significance to the resulting product. Mr. Nelson corrected this misconception individually and addressed it in activity and assessment. However, this correction did not address the fact that this student seems to have mixed up multiplication between decimals and whole numbers with the distributive property.

A study conducted by Hiebert and Wearne (1986) shows that most middle school students do not have connections between conceptual knowledge of decimals and the algorithms they learned to follow to solve decimal problems. For example, 73 percent of the students studied responded incorrectly to the problem 4 + 0.3. In the problem in figure 10.12, the student seems to have memorized rules for multiplication of decimals without understanding the specific concepts of mixed numbers, decimals, and the distributive property.

One way to address this error pattern is to help students develop better number sense of the relationship between decimals and rational numbers, specifically by using equivalent rational numbers. For instance, understanding that 0.04 = 4/100 would allow students to rewrite the decimal multiplication as

$$12(5 + 0.04) = 12\left(5 + \frac{4}{100}\right) = 12 \times 5 + 12 \times \frac{4}{100} = 60 + \frac{48}{100} = 60.48.$$

Conclusion

To understand students' thinking at a deeper "in process" level, teachers can analyze errors from representative samples of students' homework. Analyzing errors plays a vital role in gaining insight into students' thinking, particularly their misconceptions. This study investigated a strategic sampling method of grading homework that required teachers to analyze error patterns and make instructional decisions on the basis of a representative sample of six to nine student papers. The results showed that through conducting error analysis in this way, teachers were able to increase their knowledge of, and attention to, students' thinking; find patterns of errors; correct misconceptions; and guide their instruction. Research from the National Research Council (2001) supports this approach to "in process" assessment, recognizing that "effective instruction with rational numbers needs to take these errors into account" (p. 238).

The error patterns involving students' work with rational numbers revealed in this study have been identified by previous studies (Ashlock 2006; Hiebert and Wearne 1986; Sowder and Markovits 1989; Sowder 1989; Wu and An 2005). The findings from this body of work—corroborated by teachers' experiences in the classroom—suggest that children have a great deal of difficulty in developing procedural fluency and conceptual understanding while learning rational numbers. One message from our study is that to master rational number operations, students need to first make sense of rational numbers conceptually and then work toward developing procedural fluency. As part of this process, students need to see multiple representations of operations with rational numbers to help them make sense of the meaning of both the numbers with which they are working and the algorithms they apply to them.

Students need to first make sense of rational numbers conceptually and then work toward developing procedural fluency. As part of this process, students need to see multiple representations of operations with rational numbers to help them make sense of the meaning of both the numbers with which they are working and the algorithms they apply to them.

The process of error analysis can contribute to developing efficient teaching strategies if time is spent examining how and why students make mistakes, and in making corrections of the errors in a timely manner (Pajares 2002). The process of error analysis not only facilitates teachers' understanding of students' thinking but also helps students in active learning. It serves the role of nipping misconceptions in the bud before they are reinforced through repeated practice and, over time, internalized. Students

The process of error analysis not only facilitates teachers' understanding of students' thinking but also helps students in active learning.

can avoid making error patterns permanent if the teacher can help them realize and eliminate errors at an early stage in the learning process (An 2004). With less repetition of errors, students will firmly develop proficiency with concepts and skills. Furthermore, the process of error analysis provides a mirror through which teachers are able to reflect and evaluate their effectiveness in the classroom, helping to identify their strengths and weaknesses in teaching specific concepts and skills, thereby building their professional experience and confidence.

Finally, teachers in today's classrooms face challenges from an increasing awareness that one approach does not work for all students. To meet the needs of a diverse student population, error analysis offers an effective and efficient strategy that not only allows teachers to examine the work from students with different levels of proficiency and to know their different responses to instruction but also helps teachers develop multiple ways to address misconceptions that help students in linguistically and culturally diverse classrooms make better sense of mathematics.

REFERENCES

An, Shuhua. "A Comparative Study of Mathematics Programs in the U.S. and China: The Pedagogical Content Knowledge of Middle School Mathematics Teachers in the U.S. and China." Ph.D. diss., Texas A&M University, 2000.

———. *The Middle Path in Math Instruction: Solutions for Improving Math Education.* Lanham, Md.: Scarecrow Education, 2004.

An, Shuhua, and Zhonghe Wu. *Teaching Elementary and Middle School Mathematics Proficiently and Effectively.* Thousand Oaks, Calif.: Sage Publications, 2009.

Ashlock, Robert B. *Error Patterns in Computation.* Upper Saddle River, N.J.: Pearson Merrill Prentice Hall, 2006.

Bennett, Albert B., and Leonard T. Nelson. *Mathematics for Elementary Teachers: A Conceptual Approach.* Boston: McGraw Hill Higher Education, 2004.

Cathcart, W. George, Yvonne M. Pothier, James H. Vance, and Nadine S. Bezuk. *Learning Mathematics in Elementary and Middle Schools.* Upper Saddle River, N.J.: Merrill Prentice Hall, 2001.

Hiebert, James, and Diana Wearne. "Procedures over Concepts: The Acquisition of Decimal Number Knowledge. In *Conceptual and Procedural Knowledge: The Case of Mathematics,* edited by James Hiebert, pp. 199–223. Hillsdale, N.J.: Lawrence Erlbaum Associates, 1986.

Huinker, DeAnn. "Examining Dimensions of Fraction Operation Sense." In *Making Sense of Fractions, Ratios, and Proportions,* 2002 Yearbook of the National Council of Teachers of Mathematics (NCTM), edited by Bonnie Litwiller and George Bright, pp. 72–78. Reston, Va.: NCTM, 2002.

National Research Council. *Adding It Up: Helping Children Learn Mathematics.* Washington, D.C.: National Academy Press, 2001.

Pajares, Frank. "Gender and Perceived Self-Efficacy in Self-Regulated Learning." *Theory into Practice* 41, no. 2 (2002): 116–25.

Sowder, Judith T. "Mental Computation and Number Comparison: Their Roles in the Development of Number Sense and Computational Estimation." In *Number Concepts and Operations in the Middle Grades,* edited by James Hebert and Merlyn Behr, pp. 182–97. Reston, Va.: National Council of Teachers of Mathematics, 1988.

Sowder, Judith T., and Zvia Markovits. "Effects of Instruction on Number Magnitude." In *Proceedings of the Eleventh Annual Meeting of the North American Chapter of the International Group for Psychology in Mathematics Education,* edited by Carolyn A. Maher, Gerald A. Goldin, and Robert B. Davis, pp. 105–10. New Brunswick, N.J.: Rutgers University, 1989.

Wu, Zhonghe, and Shuhua An. "Developing Proficiency in Fraction Operations: Chinese Computational Strategies." Paper presented at 83rd Annual Meeting of the National Council of Teachers of Mathematics, Anaheim, Calif., April 2005.

Two additional titles appear in the
Mathematics for Every Student
series

(Carol E. Malloy, series editor):

- ***Mathematics for Every Student: Responding to Diversity, Grades Pre-K–5,*** edited by Dorothy Y. White

- ***Mathematics for Every Student: Responding to Diversity, Grades 9–12,*** edited by Alfinio Flores